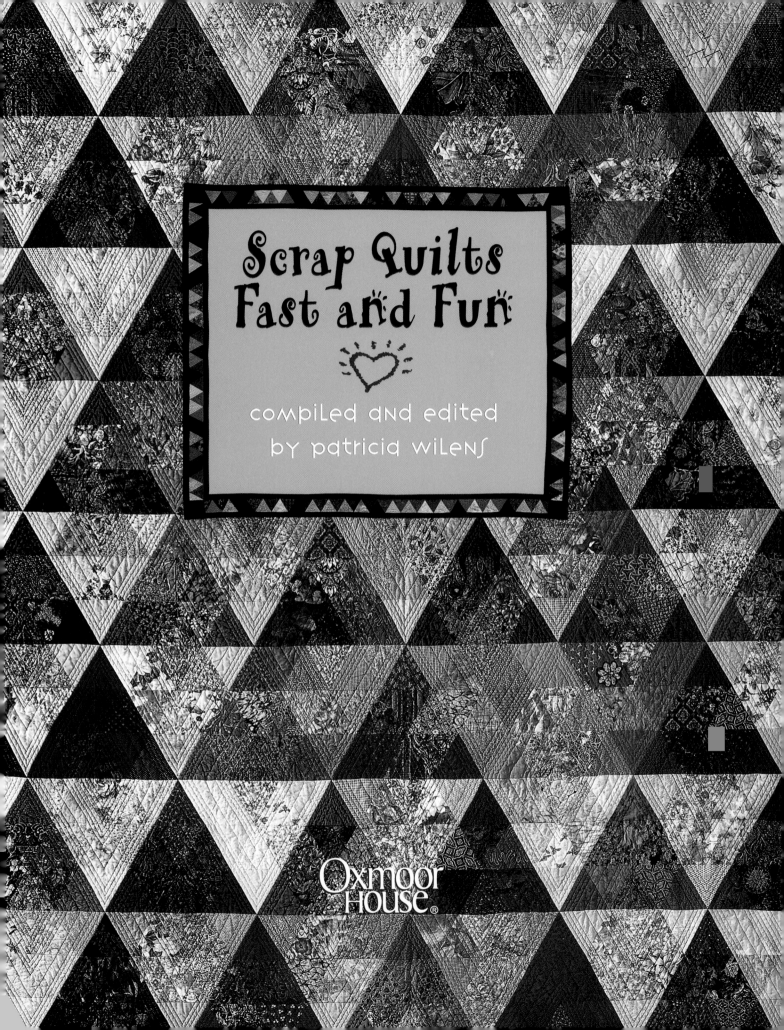

Scrap Quilts Fast and Fun

compiled and edited
by patricia wilens

Oxmoor
HOUSE®

Scrap Quilts Fast and Fun
from the *For the Love of Quilting* series
©1997 by Oxmoor House, Inc.
Book Division of
Southern Progress Corporation
P.O. Box 2463, Birmingham, Alabama 35201

Published by Oxmoor House, Inc., and Leisure Arts, Inc.

Library of Congress Catalog Card
Number: 97-68506
Hardcover ISBN: 0-8487-1670-1
Softcover ISBN: 0-8487-1671-X
Manufactured in the United States of America
First Printing 1997

Editor-in-Chief: Nancy Fitzpatrick Wyatt
Senior Crafts Editor: Susan Ramey Cleveland
Senior Editor, Editorial Services: Olivia Kindig Wells
Art Director: James Boone

Scrap Quilts Fast and Fun
Editor: Patricia Wilens
Copy Editor: Susan S. Cheatham
Editorial Assistants: Barzella Estle,
Allison D. Ingram
Associate Art Director: Cynthia R. Cooper
Designers: Carol O. Loria,
Emily Albright Parrish
Illustrator: Kelly Davis
Senior Photographer: John O'Hagan
Contributing Photographer: Keith Harrelson
Photo Stylists: Katie Stoddard,
Linda Baltzell Wright
Production Director: Phillip Lee
Associate Production Manager: Theresa L. Beste
Production Assistant: Faye Porter Bonner

We're Here For You!
Oxmoor House is dedicated to serving you with
reliable information that expands your imagination
and enriches your life. We welcome your comments
and suggestions. Please write to us at:
Oxmoor House
Editor, *Scrap Quilts Fast and Fun*
2100 Lakeshore Drive
Birmingham, AL 35209

To order additional publications, call
1-205-877-6560.

CONTENTS

Quilts

PinPoints

Step-by-Step Guide to Quiltmaking

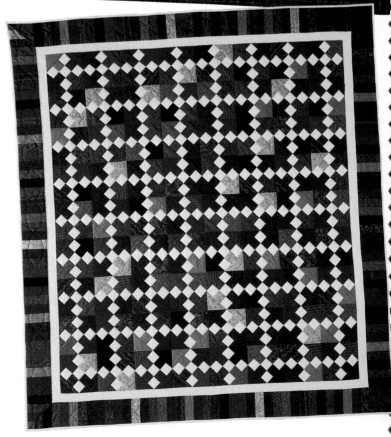

iNtroductioN

My one and only antique quilt is a scrap quilt. Its tiny basket blocks feature typical 1880s fabrics—little prints and plaids—set with a cheerful red check fabric that warms my soul.

I wonder about old quilts. The dealer who sold me my quilt thought it was made in the Midwest between 1885 and 1900. Who was the woman who made it? Are the fabrics bits of her dresses? Was she a young bride in Iowa or a Kansas grandmother? Are the blocks small because she didn't have many scraps or because she liked her blocks small and cute?

It wasn't stylish then for a quiltmaker to sign her work. A quilt was deemed ordinary woman's work and thus unworthy of grand ideas like heritage and posterity. Future generations won't find women of the 1990s so silent. It's common now to find a patch on the back of a quilt that records who made the quilt, when, where, and why—a legacy to the future.

When you make one of the quilts in this book, you become part of that legacy. These quilts mix traditional design with today's wonderful fabrics. New tools and techniques for cutting and piecing add spice to the blend.

I'd like to know the woman who made my quilt. I can tell she wasn't much for hand quilting and that's one of several things we seem to have in common. We like to sew, we love quilts (especially scrap quilts), and we're charmed by cheery red fabric. She is my sister. I wish I knew her name.

Patricia Wilens
Editor

courtHouse steps

Appearances are deceiving in this striking quilt. The design looks like a complex assembly of Japanese lanterns, but it is really *sew* easy to make. Can you find the block? Here's a hint—each black square is the *center* of one block. You'll want a mix of large-, medium-, and small-scale prints, as well as varied color, to make a quilt with interesting texture.

Finished Size

Quilt: 79" x 89½"
Blocks: 42 blocks, 10½" x 10½"
This quilt fits a full-size bed. See Size Variations (page 7) for other size requirements.

Materials

Three 1" x 42" strips *each* of 84 print fabrics
Assorted scraps for appliqué
27" square green fabric for vine
¼ yard blue fabric for bird appliqués
3 yards black solid fabric
5½ yards backing fabric
82" x 97" precut batting
½"-wide bias pressing bar

Quilt by Marion Roach Watchinski of Overland Park, Kansas

Plan Ahead

This block is easy to sew, but it takes planning to achieve the overall design. Use the **Planning Diagram** at right to map out your quilt so you can enjoy sewing without worrying about what goes where. Make several photocopies to try different arrangements.

Sort your fabrics into color groups; then get a colored marker to match each group. For example, say you have four yellow fabrics. The diagram shows each block, which is visually divided into quadrants. Choose any quadrant, on any block, and color it yellow. Then color the *adjacent* quadrant in the *adjacent* block. Repeat three times, spacing four yellow "lanterns" randomly around the quilt. When you color a quadrant on the outside edge, choose a second quadrant on another edge. Repeat with each color until you've positioned each fabric.

Use the diagram as a guide as you sew the blocks, matching fabrics in neighboring quadrants. It doesn't matter which fabric you use in any position as long as adjacent quadrants match.

Making Blocks

For this stitch-and-cut method, it is not necessary to make templates for the "steps."

1. From black fabric, cut two 2"-wide cross-grain strips. From these, cut 42 (2") A squares.
2. Select the four sets of fabric strips for Block 1A. Strips are sewn in numerical order as shown on **Block Diagram**. For first step, match fabric strip to one side of square, right sides together, and stitch **(Diagram A)**. Trim strip even with bottom of square. Press seam allowance toward step.
3. Repeat with second fabric on opposite side of square **(Diagram B)**.

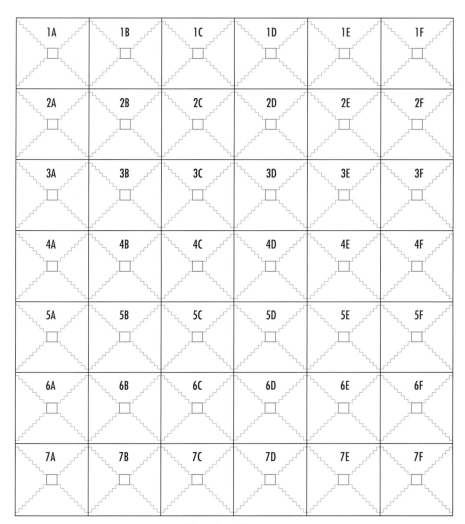

Planning Diagram

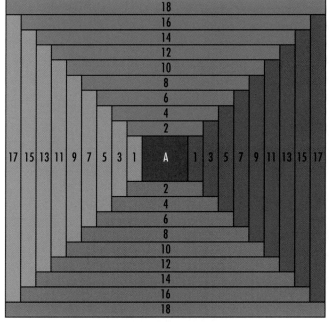

Courthouse Steps Block

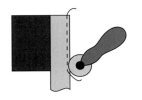

Diagram A

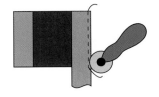

Diagram B

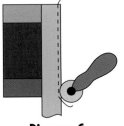

Diagram C

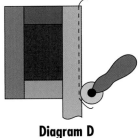

Diagram D

4. Referring to **Planning Diagram**, turn block so sewn steps are at top and bottom of square. With right sides facing, match next fabric strip to square edge and stitch (**Diagram C**). Trim strip even with bottom step and press. (*Note:* Throughout block assembly, always press seam allowances toward newest step.)

5. Turn unit so last step is at left. With right sides facing, match fourth fabric strip to remaining edge of square and stitch (**Diagram D**). Trim strip and press.

6. Continue adding steps in this manner until you have nine steps on all sides of center square (**Block Diagram**). Completed block will measure approximately 11" square.

7. In this manner, make 42 Courthouse Steps blocks.

Quilt Assembly

Throughout assembly, refer to **Planning Diagram** to keep fabrics positioned correctly.

1. Lay out seven rows, with six blocks in each row. Check position of fabrics. When satisfied with placement, join blocks in each row.

2. Lay out rows in order. Check placement of blocks again; then join rows in numerical order to assemble quilt.

Border

Appliqué patterns are on pages 9 and 10.

1. From black fabric, cut four 8½" x 94" lengthwise strips. Referring to pages 150 and 151, measure quilt and trim border strips as needed. Sew strips to quilt and miter corners.

2. See page 156 for tips on making continuous bias. Use green fabric to make 9¾ yards of 1½"-wide continuous bias. From this, cut four 88"-long strips for appliqué.

3. See page 134 for tips on bias appliqué. Fold, stitch, and press bias strips with pressing bar. Prepared vines should be ½" wide.

4. On seam line of one border strip, place pins at both corners and center. Midway between center and each corner, place two more pins on *outside edge* of border.

5. Fold one bias strip in half to find center. Pin center of vine at center of border, ¾" above seam. Working out from center, pin vine in place, curving bias up toward next pin and down again toward corner pin. Edge of vine should be ¾" above or below a marked point. Pin ends of vine at mitered seam, but don't trim excess until flowers and leaves are in place.

6. Repeat vine placement on remaining three borders.

7. Cut four B flowers, four C leaves, and four I birds from scrap fabrics, and prepare pieces for appliqué. Referring to photo on page 8, pin Bs and Cs in place at corners, covering ends of vine. Pin a bird at center of each strip, with its feet about ½" above vine.

Size Variations

	Twin	Queen	King
Finished Size	68½" x 89½"	89½" x 100"	100" x 100"
Number of Blocks	35	56	64
Blocks Set	5 x 7	7 x 8	8 x 8
Yardage Required			
Sets of scrap strips for blocks	70	112	176
Black fabric	3 yards	3⅜ yards	3⅜ yards
Backing fabric	5½ yards	8¼ yards	9¼ yards

8. From scraps, cut 28 D leaves, eight sets of H flower petals, and eight each of E, F, G, J, K, and L. Prepare pieces for appliqué. Pin two of each flower on each border, layering E/F and J/K/L as shown on patterns. Place Ds randomly as shown.

9. When satisfied with placement of vine and appliqué pieces, appliqué. Trim ends of vine as needed before stitching corner flowers.

Quilting and Finishing

1. Mark quilting design on quilt top as desired. Quilt shown has an allover fan design quilted on the blocks, 1"-square cross-hatching quilted in borders, and outline quilting around appliqué pieces.

2. Divide backing into two equal lengths. Cut one piece in half lengthwise. Join a narrow panel to each side of wide piece to assemble backing.

3. Layer backing, batting, and quilt top. Baste. Quilt as desired.

4. Use remaining black fabric to make 9⅝ yards of straight-grain binding. See page 156 for instructions on making and applying binding.

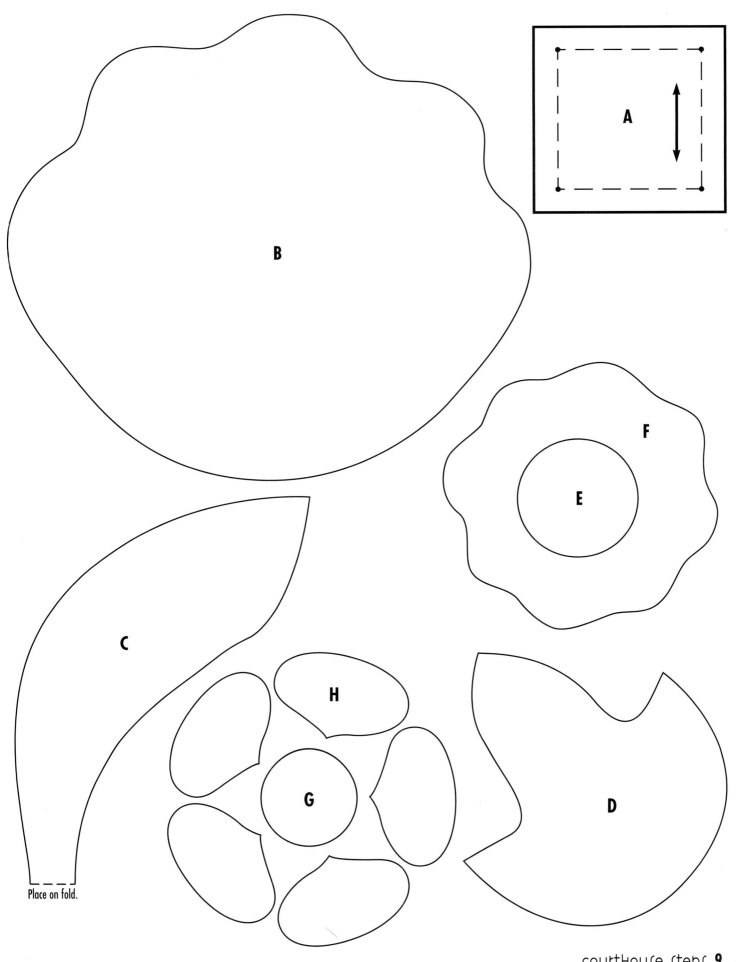

A

B

C

Place on fold.

D

E

F

G

H

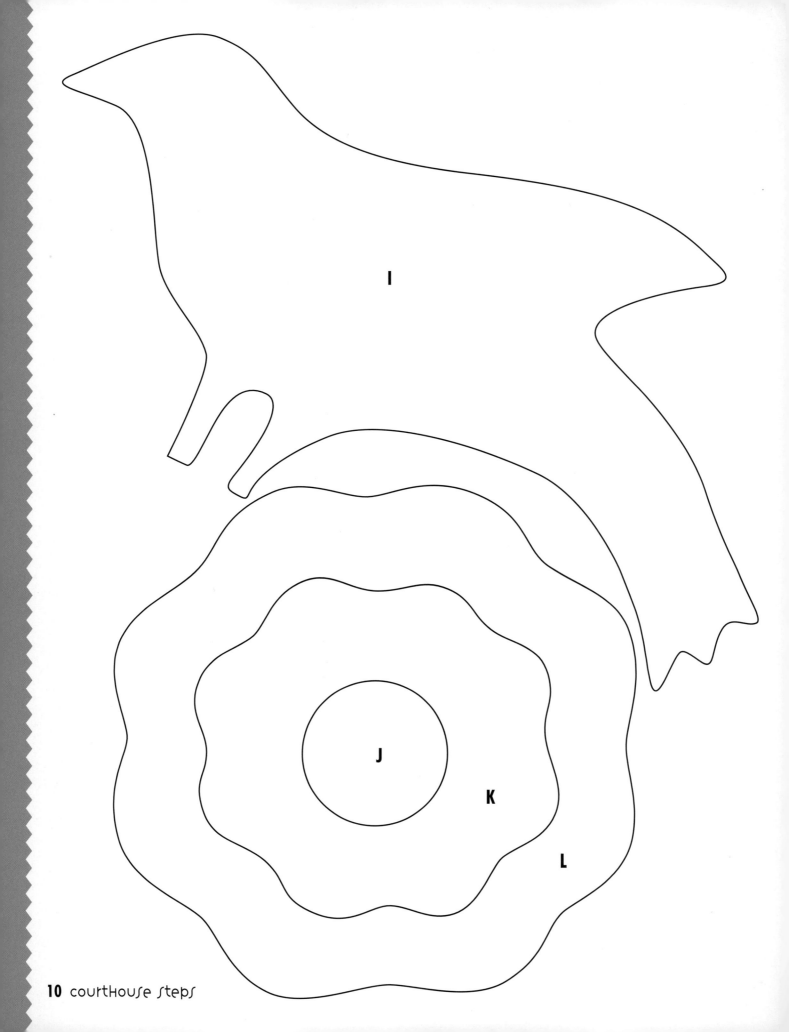

I

J

K

L

diamond jubilee

A **charm quilt's** patches are all the same shape and size, but no two are cut from the same fabric. Even if some fabrics repeat here, this quilt has charm to spare. Pieced stars hide amid the profusion of these fabrics, but you can use high-contrast fabrics to bring them out. This design is ideal for quilters who enjoy the challenge of sewing set-in seams.

Finished Size

Quilt: 82" x 91"
Blocks: 18 blocks, 15¾" x 18"
This quilt fits a full-size or queen-size bed. See Size Variations (page 16) for other size requirements.

Materials

240 (2½" x 4½") dark scraps
488 (2½" x 4½") medium scraps
248 (2½" x 4½") light scraps
3 yards border fabric
⅞ yard binding fabric
5½ yards backing fabric
90" x 108" precut batting

Quilt by Annette Anderson of Ferndale, Washington

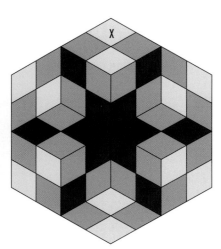

Star Block—Make 18.

Unit 1—Make 120.

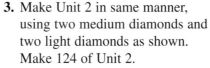

Unit 2—Make 124.

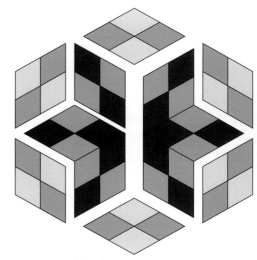

Block Assembly Diagram

Making Blocks

Instructions are for traditional piecing. The scrappy nature of this quilt makes quick piecing inappropriate. Make templates for patterns X, Y, and Z on page 16. Template Z is same as Y without seam allowance on short leg of triangle.

1. Sort fabrics by value into groups of light, medium, and dark. Use Template X to cut 240 dark, 488 light, and 248 medium diamonds. Mark seam allowance on wrong sides of each diamond.
2. Select four diamonds—two dark and two medium—for Unit 1. Join diamonds in dark/medium pairs as shown **(Diagram A)**; then join pairs to complete unit. Make 120 of Unit 1.

3. Make Unit 2 in same manner, using two medium diamonds and two light diamonds as shown. Make 124 of Unit 2.
4. For one block, select six each of units 1 and 2. Join three of Unit 1 as shown to make half-stars, sewing only from dot to dot of marked seam allowance **(Block Assembly Diagram)**. Be sure to leave ¼" unstitched at both ends of each seam. (See Sewing a Set-in Seam, page 14.)
5. Stitch center seam to complete star.

6. Set-in six of Unit 2 around star to complete block.
7. Make 18 star blocks.
8. For a half-block, join three of Unit 1 in a half-star as before. Set-in two of Unit 2 as shown **(Half-Block Assembly Diagram)**. Then sew two more of Unit 2 to remaining edges of half-star; trim these units even with unstitched edge of star as shown. Make four half-blocks.

Diagram A

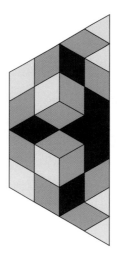

Half-Block—Make 4.

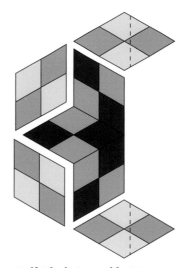

Half-Block Assembly Diagram

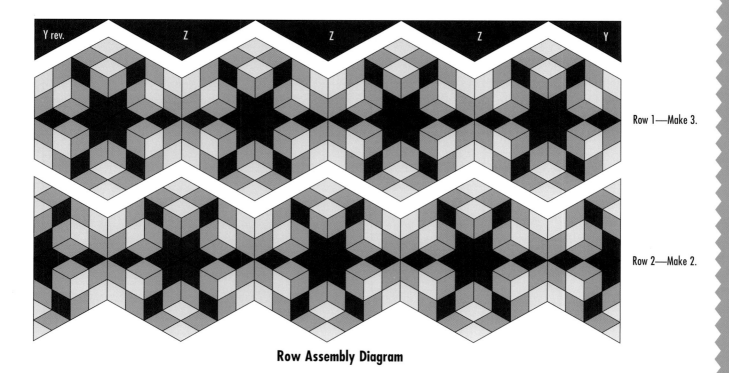

Row 1—Make 3.

Row 2—Make 2.

Row Assembly Diagram

Quilt Assembly

1. For Row 1, join four blocks as shown **(Row Assembly Diagram)**. Do not to sew beyond marked seam lines, leaving seam allowances free for setting in. Make three of Row 1.

2. In same manner, join three blocks and two half-blocks for Row 2 as shown. Make two of Row 2.

3. Referring to photo on page 15, join rows in 1-2-1-2-1 sequence, carefully sewing set-in seams.

4. Cut two 8"-wide cross-grain strips of border fabric. From these, cut two Y, two Y reversed, and six Z **(Diagram B)**.

5. Sew Y and Y reversed pieces to corners **(Row Assembly Diagram)**. Set-in Z pieces as shown.

Borders

1. From remaining border fabric, cut four 9½" x 86" lengthwise strips.

2. Referring to page 150, measure quilt from top to bottom and trim two borders to match length. Sew borders to quilt sides.

3. Measure quilt from side to side and trim remaining borders to match quilt width. Sew borders to top and bottom edges of quilt.

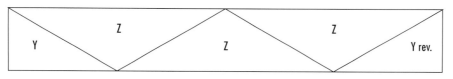

Diagram B

Quilting and Finishing

1. Mark quilting design on quilt top as desired. Quilt shown has straight-line quilting through the center of each X diamond **(Quilting Diagram)**.
2. Divide backing into two equal lengths. Cut one piece in half lengthwise. Join a narrow panel to each side of wide panel to assemble backing.
3. Layer backing, batting, and quilt top. Baste. Quilt as desired.
4. Make 10 yards of bias or straight-grain binding. See page 156 for instructions on making and applying binding.

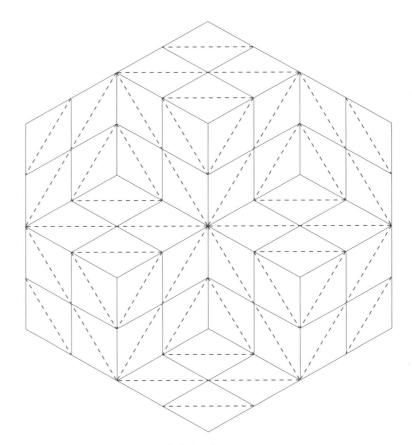

Quilting Diagram

pinpoints

Sewing a Set-in Seam

Setting patchwork pieces into an angled opening requires more than the usual accuracy in sewing. The following methods are helpful in this process. This example shows an eight-pointed diamond star, but the principles apply to other set-in shapes, too.

1 Mark corner points of seam line on each piece, using a ruler or window template. Use these matching points to align pieces when pinning. Join pieces that form an angled opening, sewing from corner point to corner point. Backstitch at beginning and end of seam, leaving seam allowances open at both ends.

To set a piece into the opening, begin by pinning one side of it in place, using corner points as a guide. Sew pinned seam between points, starting at outer edge and stopping at corner dot. Backstitch.

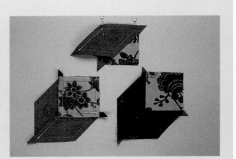

2 Realign fabric to pin adjacent side of set-in piece to opposite side of opening, right sides together. Begin sewing at inside corner dot. Stitch and backstitch, making sure stitches don't pass dot and go into seam allowance. Stitch to outside edge. Press seam allowances open or to one side, as you prefer.

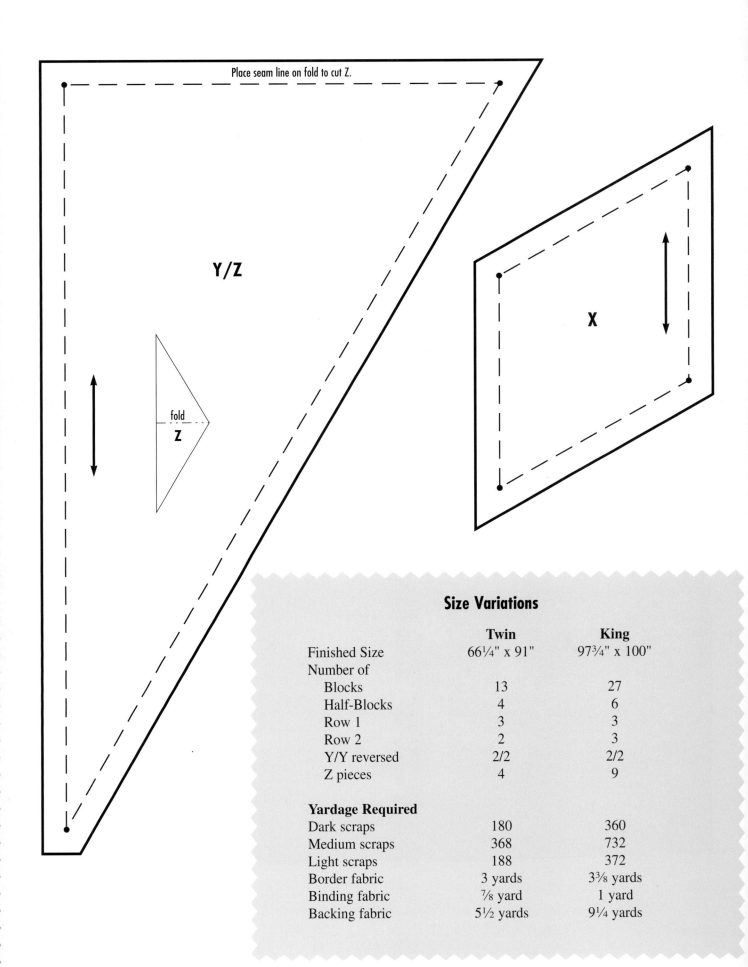

Place seam line on fold to cut Z.

Y/Z

fold
Z

X

Size Variations

	Twin	King
Finished Size	66¼" x 91"	97¾" x 100"
Number of		
Blocks	13	27
Half-Blocks	4	6
Row 1	3	3
Row 2	2	3
Y/Y reversed	2/2	2/2
Z pieces	4	9
Yardage Required		
Dark scraps	180	360
Medium scraps	368	732
Light scraps	188	372
Border fabric	3 yards	3⅜ yards
Binding fabric	⅞ yard	1 yard
Backing fabric	5½ yards	9¼ yards

madras kaLeidoscope

Careful placement of light and dark fabrics creates the kaleidoscopic effect of this quilt. Surrounded by light fabrics that seem to recede, the dark fabrics advance in bursts of color against halos of light. This quilt is a patchwork of plaids, but you can achieve a similar effect with other fabrics.

Finished Size

Quilt: 51½" x 66"
Blocks: 48 blocks, 7¼" x 7¼"
This quilt is a wall hanging or lap quilt. See Size Variations (page 19) for other size requirements.

Materials

24 (4½" x 10") dark scraps
48 (4½" x 10") medium/dark
   scraps
24 (4½" x 10") light scraps
4 (5" x 9") fabrics for border
   appliqué (optional)
48 (3" x 6") light scraps
2 yards border fabric
¾ yard binding fabric
3⅜ yards backing fabric
72" x 90" precut batting

Quilt by Peggy Ann Taggart of Janesville, Wisconsin

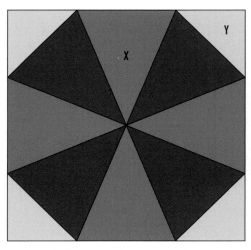

Kaleidoscope Block A—Make 24.

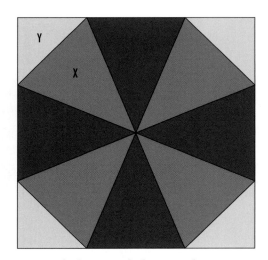

Kaleidoscope Block B—Make 24.

Making Blocks

Two blocks alternate to create the kaleidoscope look of this quilt. Block A uses dark and medium colors that dominate the overall design. Block B uses light and medium colors. Both blocks are assembled in the same manner.

For traditional cutting, make templates of patterns X and Y on page 20.

1. For Block A, select a dark fabric and a medium fabric. Cut four X triangles from each fabric. For rotary cutting, see **Cutting Diagram**.
2. Join contrasting color triangles in pairs **(Block Assembly Diagram)**.
3. Join two pairs of triangles to make a half-block. Join half-blocks. Press seam allowances toward dark triangles.
4. From one 3" x 6" light fabric, cut

two 3" squares. Cut squares in half diagonally to get four Y triangles. Sew one Y to end of each dark X to complete block.
5. Make 24 of Block A.
6. Make Block B in same manner. Use four X triangles of dark or medium-color fabric and four X triangles of a light fabric. Sew Y triangles to ends of light X triangles. Make 24 of Block B.

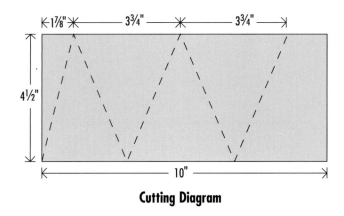

Cutting Diagram

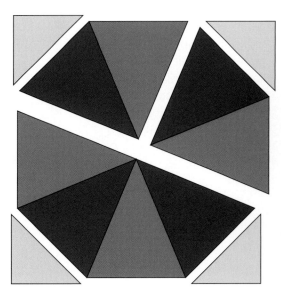

Block Assembly Diagram

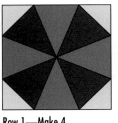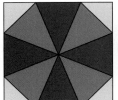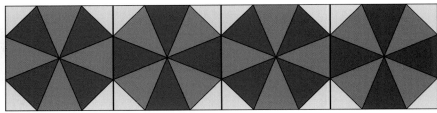

Row 1—Make 4.

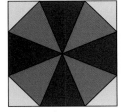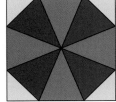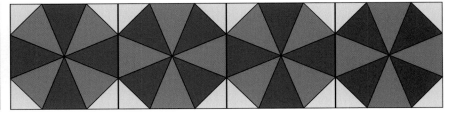

Row 2—Make 4.

Row Assembly Diagram

Quilt Assembly

1. Lay out eight horizontal rows of six blocks each, alternating A blocks and B blocks as shown (Row Assembly Diagram). Lay out four of Row 1, starting with an A block. Then lay out four of Row 2, starting with a B block. Rearrange blocks as needed to achieve a pleasing balance of color and contrast.
2. When satisfied with placement, join blocks in each row.
3. Join rows, alternating rows as shown in photo.

Border

1. From border fabric, cut four 4¼" x 72" lengthwise strips. Referring to page 150, measure quilt and trim border strips to fit as needed.
2. For embellishments, cut eight 1½" x 6½" bias strips from remaining fabrics. Turn under ¼" seam allowances on long sides of each strip and press. Appliqué strips onto borders as desired.
3. Sew borders to quilt and miter corners.

Quilting and Finishing

1. Mark quilting design on quilt top as desired. Quilt shown has outline quilting in patchwork. Straight-line quilting parallels appliquéd embellishments in borders.
2. Divide backing into two equal lengths. Cut one piece in half lengthwise. Join the two narrow panels to sides of wide panel to assemble backing.
3. Layer backing, batting, and quilt top. Backing seams will parallel top and bottom edges. Baste. Quilt as desired.
4. Make 7 yards of bias or straight-grain binding. See page 156 for instructions on making and applying binding.

Size Variations

	Twin	Full/Queen	King
Finished Size	66" x 95"	80½" x 95"	95" x 95"
Number of			
A Blocks	48	60	72
B Blocks	48	60	72
Blocks Set	8 x 12	10 x 12	12 x 12
Yardage Required			
Dark scraps	48	60	72
Medium/dark scraps	96	120	144
Light scraps	48	60	72
3" x 6" light scraps	96	120	144
Border fabric	2¾ yards	2¾ yards	2¾ yards
Binding fabric	⅞ yard	1 yard	1 yard
Backing fabric	5⅜ yards	5⅞ yards	8¾ yards

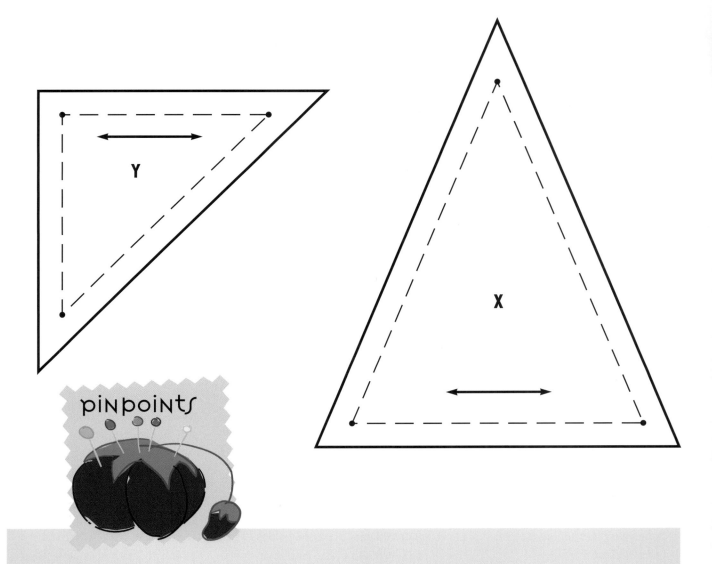

Hanging Sleeve

Hanging a quilt on the wall is a nice way to display it, but only a sturdy, lightweight quilt should be hung. If a quilt is in delicate condition, hanging will only hasten its deterioration. Protect the quilt by hanging it properly. Nails, staples, and tacks cause tearing and discoloration.

The method most often used to hang a quilt is to slip a dowel or curtain rod through a sleeve sewn to the quilt back. This method distributes the weight evenly across the width of the quilt.

To make a sleeve, cut or piece leftover backing fabric to make a strip 8" wide that is the same length as the quilt edge.

1 **Turn under** ½" on each end of the strip; then turn under another ½". Topstitch to hem both ends. With wrong sides facing, fold the fabric in half lengthwise and stitch the long edges together. Press seam allowances open and to the middle of the sleeve.

2 **Center the sleeve** on the back of the quilt about 1" below the binding with the seam against the backing. Hand-sew the sleeve to the quilt through backing and batting along both long edges. For large quilts, make two or three sleeve sections so you can use more nails or brackets to support the dowel to better distribute the quilt's weight.

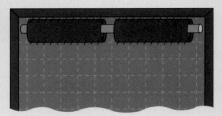

crossed canoes

Two color combinations (blue/yellow and red/green) progress from light to dark across the surface of this wall hanging. This is a great way to use up scraps in specific color families. The quilt also poses the challenge of sorting and rating fabrics by value instead of color.

Finished Size

Quilt: 42" x 42"
Blocks: 25 blocks, 6" x 6"
This quilt is a wall hanging or crib quilt. See Size Variations (page 23) for other size requirements.

Materials

25 (4½" x 12") light/medium scraps
25 (4½" x 12") dark/medium scraps
¼ yard solid border fabric
⅝ yard print border fabric
⅝ yard binding fabric
1½ yards backing fabric
45" x 60" precut batting

Quilt by Lynn Williams of Snohomish, Washington

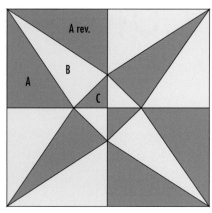

Crossed Canoes Block—Make 25.

Making Blocks

Make templates for patterns A, B, and C on page 24.

1. Start by sorting fabrics by value. In this quilt, 13 blue/yellow blocks alternate with 12 red/green blocks, each block becoming progressively darker in value. For a coordinated color scheme like this, pair the lightest fabric of each color with the lightest fabric of coordinating color and continue matching fabrics of similar value until darkest fabrics are paired. If colors are varied, pair fabrics of different colors but similar value and intensity. If you prefer, limit your fabrics to just two high-contrast colors to get a positive-negative look **(Positive-Negative Diagram)**. Select fabric pairs for 25 blocks.

2. For one block, cut two A triangles, two A triangles reversed, two Bs, and two Cs from each fabric.

3. Sew A and A reversed of one fabric to sides of each opposite fabric B as shown **(Block Assembly Diagram)**. Press all seam allowances toward same fabric.

4. Sew Cs of opposite fabric to bottom edge of each B to complete quadrant.

5. Join quadrants in pairs as shown; then join halves to complete block.

6. Make 25 Crossed Canoes blocks.

Postive-Negative Diagram

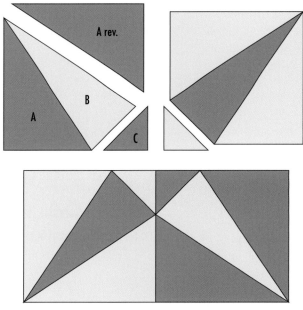

Block Assembly Diagram

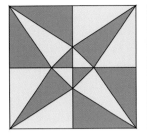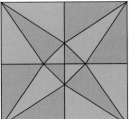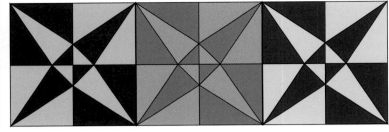

Row Assembly Diagram

Quilt Assembly

1. Lay out blocks in five horizontal rows of five blocks each **(Row Assembly Diagram)**. Start with lightest blocks at left corner of Row 1 and darkest blocks at right corner of Row 5. Rearrange blocks as desired to achieve a pleasing balance of color and value.
2. When satisfied with layout, join blocks in each row.
3. Join rows.

Borders

1. From solid border fabric, cut four 1½"-wide cross-grain strips. Referring to page 150, measure quilt from top to bottom and trim two borders to match length. Sew borders to quilt sides.
2. Measure quilt from side to side and trim remaining borders to match quilt width. Sew borders to top and bottom edges of quilt.
3. From print border fabric, cut four 5¼"-wide cross-grain strips. Sew these to quilt in same manner as for inner border.

Quilting and Finishing

1. Mark quilting design on quilt top as desired. Quilt shown is outline-quilted.
2. Layer backing, batting, and quilt top. Baste. Quilt as desired.
3. Make 5 yards of bias or straight-grain binding. See page 156 for instructions on making and applying binding.

Size Variations

	Twin	Full/Queen	King
Finished Size	66" x 96"	84" x 96"	96" x 96"
Number of Blocks	126	168	196
Blocks Set	9 x 14	12 x 14	14 x 14
Yardage Required			
Light/medium scraps	126	168	196
Medium/dark scraps	126	168	196
Solid border fabric	⅜ yard	⅜ yard	⅜ yard
Print border fabric	2½ yards	2½ yards	2⅞ yards
Binding fabric	⅞ yard	⅞ yard	1 yard
Backing fabric	5¾ yards	5¾ yards	8¾ yards

pinpoints

Backing Can Be Scrappy, Too

One reason for making scrap quilts (and there are many!) is to use up fabric. Whether a piece of fabric is old or just left over, it takes up space on the shelf and makes you feel guilty about buying new fabric.

If you're looking for a way to use up big pieces of leftover fabric, use them for backing. After all, if your quilt top is scrappy, why not make the back scrappy as well?

You can tell your friends and family that you're being frugal, since using scrap is more economical than buying more yardage (which often results in still more scrap). In addition, you can legitimately claim to be following in the great tradition of nineteenth-century quiltmakers, who made creative use of what fabric they had in a similar manner.

Piece your scraps as necessary to make a backing that is at least 3" larger on all sides than the quilt top. The backing shown here is an example of how to make good use of large pieces. The front of this quilt (*Sunflower Sayonara*, page 25) uses many red fabrics, so the leftovers make a suitable backing that has a cozy, homespun look.

Piecing a backing uses up lots of oldies, uglies, and leftovers. This gives you a good excuse to restock your shelves with wonderful new fabric!

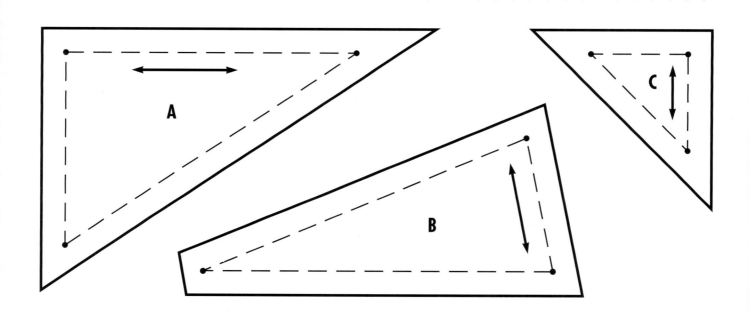

sunflower sayonara

every block in this sunny quilt is red, yellow, and green, but scrap fabrics make each block dramatically different. The blocks, made as going-away gifts by Terri Shinn's guild friends, combine piecing and appliqué. Terri's quilt tops off the color scheme with a bold coordinating border fabric. Strong color updates this design, an adaptation of a 1930s pattern.

Finished Size

Quilt: 77" x 87"
Blocks: 42 blocks, 10" x 10"
This quilt fits a full-size bed. See Size Variations (page 26) for other size requirements.

Materials

42 (11") red squares
42 (10" x 18") green scraps
42 (10") yellow squares
42 (3½" x 6") brown/black scraps
¾ yard fabric for middle border
2⅜ yards fabric for outer border
1 yard binding fabric
5½ yards backing fabric
81" x 96" precut batting

Quilt by Terri Shinn of Snohomish, Washington, from friendship blocks by the Anchorage (Alaska) Log Cabin Quilters; quilted by Tammy Christman

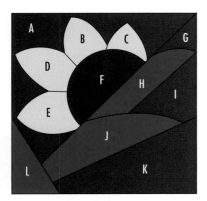

Sunflower Block—Make 42.

Making Blocks

Make templates of patterns B–L on pages 28 and 30. Use a ⅛" holepunch or a large needle to punch dots in templates as indicated on patterns.

1. Cut one red square in half diagonally to get two triangles. Set aside one triangle for A. From second triangle, cut one each of G, I, and K as shown **(Diagram A)**.

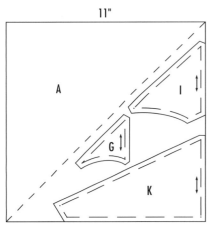

Diagram A

2. Cut a 3½" x 10" strip from one yellow fabric and set aside for border. Adding seam allowance, cut one each of B, C, D, and E from remainder of scrap. Cut one F from black scrap. Leaving bottom edges flat, turn under seam allowances on each piece.

3. Pin pieces onto A, referring to photos and diagrams for placement. Align raw edge of F with diagonal edge of A triangle, and position points of B, D, and E a scant ½" from perpendicular edges of triangle. When satisfied with placement, appliqué pieces in place in alphabetical order, overlapping subsequent pieces as shown on pattern. Press appliquéd triangle and set aside.

4. Cut a 7" x 10" strip from one green scrap and set aside for border. From remaining fabric, cut one each of H, J, and L. Mark dots on wrong side of each piece.

5. Matching dots, pin G to H. Referring to page 41 for tips on piecing curved seams, join curved edges of G and H **(Block Assembly Diagram)**, piecing by hand

Block Assembly Diagram

or machine. If you have trouble piecing this curved seam, you can turn under seam allowance on H and appliqué edge to G. Press seam allowance toward G.

6. Stitch I to bottom edge of H as shown. Press seam allowance toward I.

7. Piece or appliqué curved edge of J to bottom of H/I, matching dots. Press seam allowance toward J.

8. Stitch K to bottom edge of I/J. Press seam allowance toward K.

9. Join stem section to appliquéd triangle, aligning sections at top right corner of block (Triangle A is longer than stem section). Press seam allowance toward A.

10. Align ruler with raw edge of J/K at bottom left corner of block. With ruler in position, use a rotary cutter to trim corner of A triangle.

11. Sew L to A/J/K corner to complete block. Press seam allowance toward L.

12. Make 42 Sunflower blocks in this manner.

Size Variations

	Twin	Queen	King
Finished Size	67" x 87"	87" x 97"	97" x 97"
Number of Blocks	35	56	64
Blocks Set	5 x 7	7 x 8	8 x 8
Number of Flying Geese	44	56	60
Yardage Required			
Red scraps	35	56	64
Green scraps	35	56	64
Yellow scraps	35	56	64
Brown/black scraps	35	56	64
Middle border fabric	¾ yard	¾ yard	¾ yard
Outer border fabric	2⅜ yards	2⅝ yards	2⅞ yards
Binding fabric	1 yard	1 yard	1 yard
Backing fabric	5½ yards	8 yards	9 yards

Row Assembly Diagram

Quilt Assembly

1. Lay out seven horizontal rows with six blocks in each row **(Row Assembly Diagram)**. Rearrange blocks as desired to achieve a pleasing balance of color and value. When satisfied with placement, join blocks in each row.
2. Join rows, referring to photo on page 29.

Borders

Before cutting, read instructions and decide whether you prefer diagonal-corner quick-piecing technique or traditional piecing for flying geese. Instructions are for rotary cutting. For traditional cutting, use patterns M and N on page 28 to make templates.

1. From remaining green fabrics, cut 56 (3" x 5½") pieces to make geese with diagonal-corner technique or 56 of Template M for traditional piecing.
2. From remaining yellow fabrics, cut 104 (3") squares to make geese with diagonal-corner technique or 104 of Template N for traditional piecing.
3. Referring to page 146, use the diagonal-corner technique to sew two yellow squares to one green rectangle **(Diagram B)**. Or sew N

triangles to M triangle traditionally as shown. Make 48 flying geese.
4. Add a triangle corner to one corner only of remaining eight M pieces, sewing four left corners and four right corners as shown **(Diagram C)**.

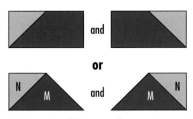

Diagram C

5. Referring to photo on page 29, join 13 flying geese end-to-end in a row for each side border. In same manner, join 11 flying geese in a row for top and bottom borders. Add a corner unit to both ends of each row.
6. Sew borders to quilt edges, easing to fit as needed. Miter border corners.
7. For middle border, cut eight 2½"-wide crosswise strips. Join two strips end-to-end to make each border.
8. Referring to page 150, measure quilt from top to bottom and trim two middle borders to match

length. Sew border strips to quilt sides.
9. Measure quilt from side to side and trim remaining middle borders to match quilt width. Sew borders to top and bottom edges of quilt.
10. From outer border fabric, cut four 4½"-wide lengthwise border strips. Measure quilt, trim, and sew outer borders as for middle borders.

Quilting and Finishing

1. Mark quilting design on quilt top as desired. Quilt shown is outline-quilted with details quilted on appliqué pieces as shown on patterns.
2. Divide backing into two equal lengths. Cut one piece in half lengthwise. Join a narrow panel to each side of wide piece to assemble backing.
3. Layer backing, batting, and quilt top. Baste. Quilt as desired.
4. Make 9⅜ yards of bias or straight-grain binding. See page 156 for instructions on making and applying binding.

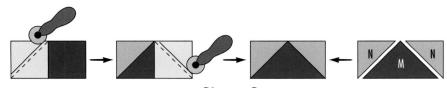

Diagram B

B

C

D

F

E

M

N

H

Color Choices

If the bright, bold colors of Terri Shinn's quilt are not quite your style, just imagine a field of sunflowers in a color scheme that suits you. To get your creative juices started, we've illustrated a couple of suggestions. At left is a soft, pastel version; at right is the look of earth tones.

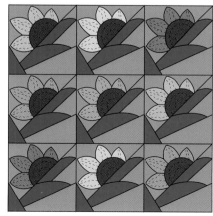

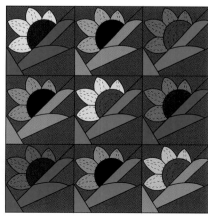

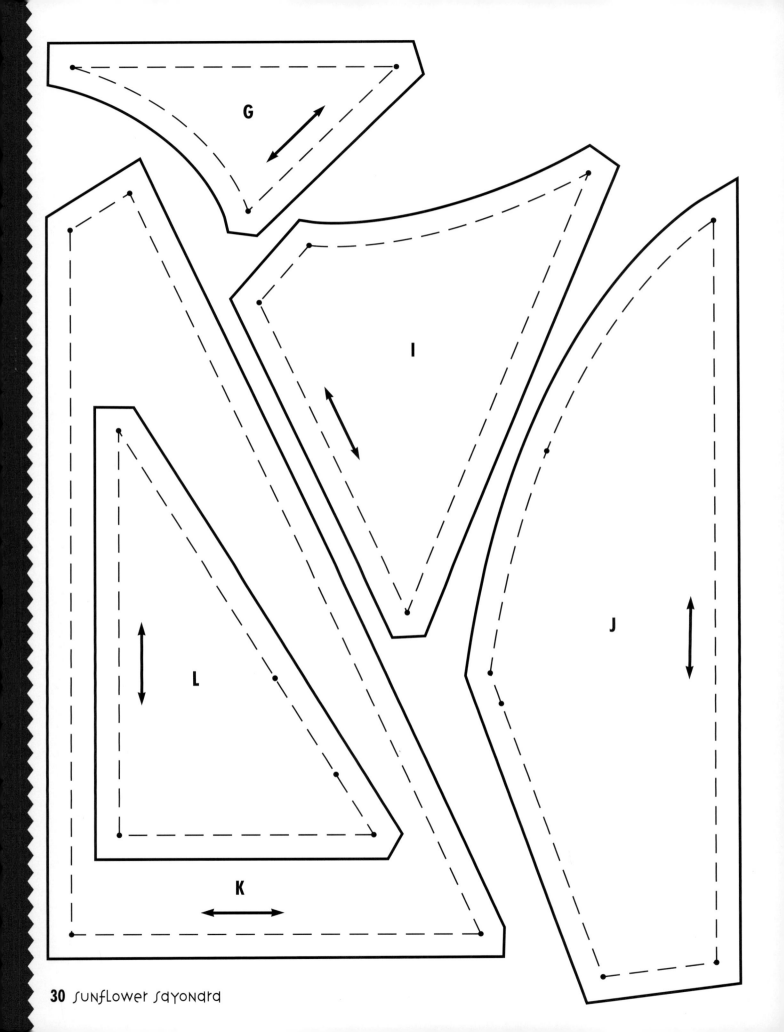

G

I

L

K

J

wildflowers

here's a recipe for success: mix one basic leaf shape and a basket of scrap fabrics. Appliqué thoroughly, add a little pinch of embroidery, and *voilà!* You have a garden that will last a lifetime. The simplest of appliqué brings life to any reproduction of this Depression-era quilt, which still blooms with old-fashioned sweetness.

Finished Size

Quilt: 61" x 75"
Blocks: 48 blocks, 7" x 7"
This quilt fits a twin-size bed. See Size Variations (page 33) for other size requirements.

Materials

48 (2" x 3½") green scraps
240 (2" x 3½") assorted scraps
¾ yard inner border fabric
3¾ yards background/outer border fabric
¾ yard binding fabric
4 yards backing fabric
72" x 90" precut batting
Embroidery floss

Antique quilt owned by Patricia Cox of Minneapolis, Minnesota

Wildflower Block—Make 48.

Making Blocks

Instructions are for hand appliqué. Make a template of Pattern A on page 34, and see page 144 for tips on cutting appliqué pieces.

1. Adding ¼" seam allowances around each piece, cut one A from green fabric and five from scrap fabrics for each block.
2. From background fabric, cut four 8" x 63" lengthwise strips for outer borders. Set aside. From remaining background fabric, cut 48 (7½") squares. Fold each background square in half diagonally and crease to establish diagonal center line.
3. Center one square over pattern on page 34, aligning edges and center crease with stem embroidery line. Lightly trace outline of block on fabric.
4. Turn under seam allowances on A pieces. Referring to pattern, pin

Four-Block Diagram

pieces in place. Petals will overlap slightly at center of flower. When satisfied with position of pinned pieces, appliqué in place.
5. Use two strands of embroidery floss to work stem and vine in backstitch. Cover ends of petals at center with satin stitch. (See stitch diagrams on page 34.)
6. Appliqué and embroider 48 blocks.

Quilt Assembly

1. For ease of assembly, join blocks in groups of four so green leaves meet at center (**Four-Block Diagram**). Make 12 four-block units.
2. Referring to photo on page 31, lay out four-block units in four horizontal rows with three units in each row (**Row Assembly Diagram**). Arrange units in rows to achieve a pleasing balance of color and contrast.
3. Join units in each row. Join rows.

Borders

1. Cut eight 2½"-wide crosswise strips from fabric for inner border. Join two strips end-to-end to make each border strip.
2. Referring to page 150, measure quilt from top to bottom and trim two borders to match length. Sew border strips to quilt sides.
3. Measure quilt from side to side and trim remaining inner borders to match quilt width. Sew borders to top and bottom edges of quilt.
4. Measure quilt, trim, and sew outer borders in same manner.

Quilting and Finishing

1. Mark quilting design on quilt top as desired. On quilt shown, flowers and blocks are outline-quilted and a 1"-wide diagonal cross-hatching is quilted in borders.
2. Divide backing into two equal lengths. Cut one piece in half lengthwise. Join a narrow panel to each side of wide piece to assemble backing.
3. Layer backing, batting, and quilt top. (Backing seams will run parallel to top and bottom edges.) Baste. Quilt as desired.
4. Make 8 yards of 2½"-wide bias or straight-grain binding. See page 156 for instructions on making and applying binding.

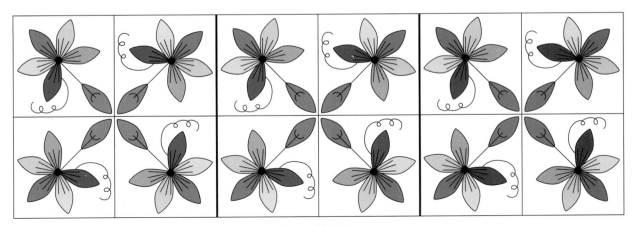

Row Assembly Diagram

Another Look

Stretch your imagination to create a new block with these patterns. Here's our suggestion for a Wildflowers quilt that's a little different. Standing up straight, the same flower fits a block approximately 5½" x 9" (finished size).

Your choice of color scheme will make your quilt unique. Consider light, bright flowers on a dark background, or pale blooms on mottled blue for the look of water lilies. So many possibilities, not enough time!

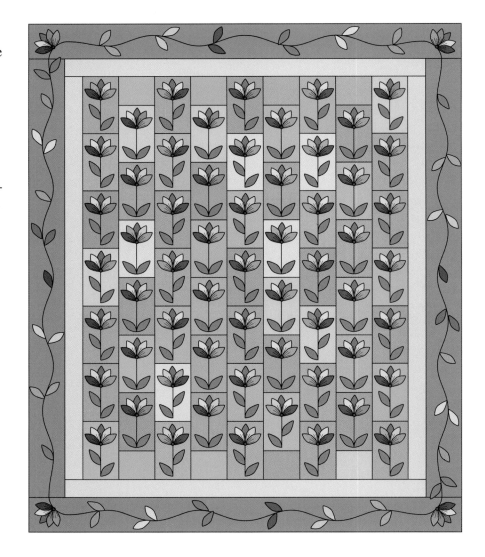

Size Variations

	Full	Queen	King
Finished Size	75" x 89"	89" x 103"	103" x 103"
Number of Blocks	80	120	144
Blocks Set	8 x 10	10 x 12	12 x 12
Yardage Required			
Assorted scraps	400	600	720
Green scraps	80	120	144
Inner border fabric	¾ yard	¾ yard	¾ yard
Background fabric	5¼ yards	7⅛ yards	8¼ yards
Binding fabric	⅞ yard	1 yard	1 yard
Backing fabric	4¾ yards	8¼ yards	9¼ yards

Satin stitch. Starting at top of circle, bring needle up on one side and insert it on opposite side. Carry thread behind work to repeat, stitching from one side to the other. Keep stitches parallel, smooth, and close together.

Satin Stitch

Backstitch. Working from right to left, or top to bottom, bring needle up on drawn guideline. Take a stitch backward and bring needle up an equal distance ahead of first hole made by thread. Repeat, taking needle back to end of previous stitch.

Backstitch

pyramids

A **skillful blend**
of hue and
value, this
easy-to-sew
quilt contrasts busy prints
with subtle tone-on-tone
fabrics in each triangular
block. To expand your
fabric selection, exchange
scraps with friends. It's
fun, and you can all make
quilts together.

Finished Size

Quilt: 85½" x 93¼"
Blocks:
88 blocks, 9⅞" x 11⅞"
This quilt fits a queen-size
bed. Because of the pieced
border, size variations are
not recommended for this
quilt.

Materials

Print scrap fabrics in blue,
green, purple, brown,
red, and gold (see Sort-
ing Fabrics, page 36,
for more information)
2⅝ yards black mini-print
8 yards backing fabric
90" x 108" precut batting

Quilt by Lyn D. Johnson of Columbia, South Carolina

Sorting Fabrics

To achieve the look of Lyn Johnson's quilt, you'll need to sort fabrics by color, value, and texture. Each block is a combination of multicolor prints and tone-on-tones. For each dark block, you'll make a corresponding light block of the same color family.

Start by sorting fabrics into color families—blue, green, gold, brown, red, and purple. Some fabrics could go into more than one group. For example, is teal a blue or a green? If you have enough blue-green fabrics, make that a new color family. If you have only a few, mix them into both groups.

Next, sort each color family into lights and darks. Most fabrics clearly fall into one group or the other. Mediums can go in either group, because these adapt to the lightness or darkness of surrounding fabrics.

The last sort is for texture. Separate each group into large or multicolor prints and tone-on-tone prints.

When you're done sorting, you should have at least 24 separated groups of fabric. (Use zip-top bags or plastic boxes to keep them sorted.) Cutting instructions below list how many triangles to cut from each group.

Cutting

For traditional cutting, use patterns A, B, and C on page 38 to make templates. For rotary cutting, cut scrap fabrics into 4"-wide strips. Align 60° angles on rotary-cutting ruler with bottom edge of strip to cut equilateral triangles (Diagrams A and B).

From large prints, cut:
- 48 As, 5 Bs, and 4 Bs reversed of brown.
- 48 As, 4 Bs, and 5 Bs reversed of beige (light brown).

- 58 As of dark blue.
- 56 As of light blue.
- 72 As each of dark green and light green.
- 72 As, 4 Bs, and 5 Bs reversed of dark red/red-violet.
- 72 As, 4 Bs, and 4 Bs reversed of pink (light red).
- 30 As of dark purple.
- 24 As each of light purple, dark gold and yellow (light gold).

From tone-on-tone fabrics, cut:
- 25 As, 2 Bs, and 2 Bs reversed of brown.
- 23 As, 2 Bs, and 2 Bs reversed of beige.
- 34 As of dark blue.
- 31 As, 1 B, and 1 B reversed of light blue.
- 46 As and 1 B of dark green.
- 44 As of light green.
- 47 As, 2 Bs, and 2 Bs reversed of dark red/red violet.
- 42 As, 2 Bs, and 2 Bs reversed of pink.
- 19 As and 1 B reversed of dark purple.
- 22 As of light purple.
- 23 As and 1 B of dark gold.
- 19 As of yellow.

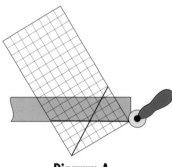

Diagram A

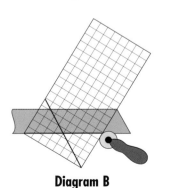

Diagram B

Making Blocks

1. For one block, select six print triangles and three tone-on-tone triangles of the same color and value (for example, light blue).
2. Join print triangles in two rows of three triangles each as shown (Diagram C). Join rows.

Diagram C

3. Sew tone-on-tone triangles to three sides of center unit to complete block as shown (Diagram D). Press.

Diagram D

4. In this manner, make two blocks each of dark purple, light purple, gold, and yellow; six blocks each of brown and beige; eight blocks each of dark blue and light blue; 12 blocks each of dark green and light green; and 10 blocks each of red and pink.
5. Make half-blocks in same manner. Make four each of red or red-violet, pink, brown, and beige. Make half of each set with two Bs and one B reversed (Diagram E, left); make second pair of half-blocks with one B and two Bs reversed (Diagram E, right).

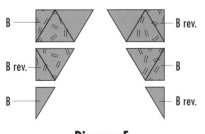

B — B rev.

B rev. — B

B — B rev.

Diagram E

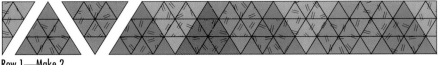
Row 1—Make 2.

Row 2—Make 2.

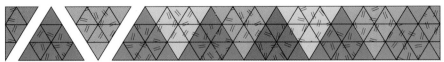
Row 3—Make 2.

Row 4—Make 2.

Row Assembly Diagram

Quilt Assembly

Refer to photo on page 35 and **Row Assembly Diagram** throughout.

1. For Row 1, select two blocks each of dark blue and pink, three blocks each of dark green and beige, one dark purple block, and two pink half-blocks. Starting with half-block at left side, join blocks as shown. Make two of Row 1.

2. For Row 2, select two blocks each of gold and light blue, three blocks each of light green and red, one light purple block, and two brown half-blocks. Join blocks as shown. Make two of Row 2.

3. For Row 3, select two blocks each of dark blue and yellow, three blocks each of dark green and pink, one dark purple block, and two beige half-blocks. Join blocks as shown. Make two of Row 3.

4. For Row 4, select two blocks each of light blue and red, three blocks each of light green and brown, one light purple block, and two red half-blocks. Join

blocks as shown. Make two of Row 4.

5. Referring to photo, join rows 1-2-3-4. Assemble second set of rows 1-2-3-4. Join Row 4 of first set to Row 1 of second set.

Borders

1. From black fabric, cut eight 2½"-wide lengthwise strips. Set aside four strips for outer border. Referring to page 150, measure quilt and trim remaining strips for inner border. Sew border strips to quilt edges with square corners.

2. For middle border, join remaining A triangles in 14 groups of five, consisting of two lights and three darks per group (**Diagram F**). Make eight units with B triangles for corners (**Diagram G**). Make four nine-triangle units with four lights and five darks (**Diagram H**).

3. From black fabric, cut 22 A triangles and four 3¾" C squares.

4. For top border, select any five five-triangle units, two corner units, and six black As. Referring to photo, lay out units in a row, with black triangles between units

and dark fabrics at bottom. When satisfied with placement, join units. Sew border to top edge of quilt, easing as necessary.

5. Make bottom border in same manner.

6. For each side border, join two nine-triangle units, two five-triangle units, two corner units, and five black triangles as shown. Sew black squares to border ends. Sew borders to quilt sides, easing as necessary.

7. For outer border, measure and trim remaining black strips to quilt edges. Sew borders to quilt with square corners.

Quilting and Finishing

1. Mark quilting design on quilt top as desired. Quilt shown has echo quilting in each block and half-block (**Quilting Pattern**). Black borders are outline-quilted.

2. Divide backing into three equal lengths. Cut one piece in half lengthwise and discard one narrow panel. Join wide panels to both sides of remaining narrow piece to assemble backing.

3. Layer backing, batting, and quilt top. Baste. Quilt as desired.

4. Use remaining black fabric to make 10 yards of bias or straight-grain binding. See page 156 for instructions on making and applying binding.

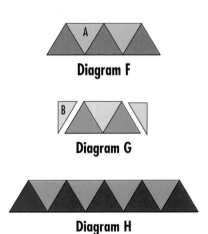
Diagram F

Diagram G

Diagram H

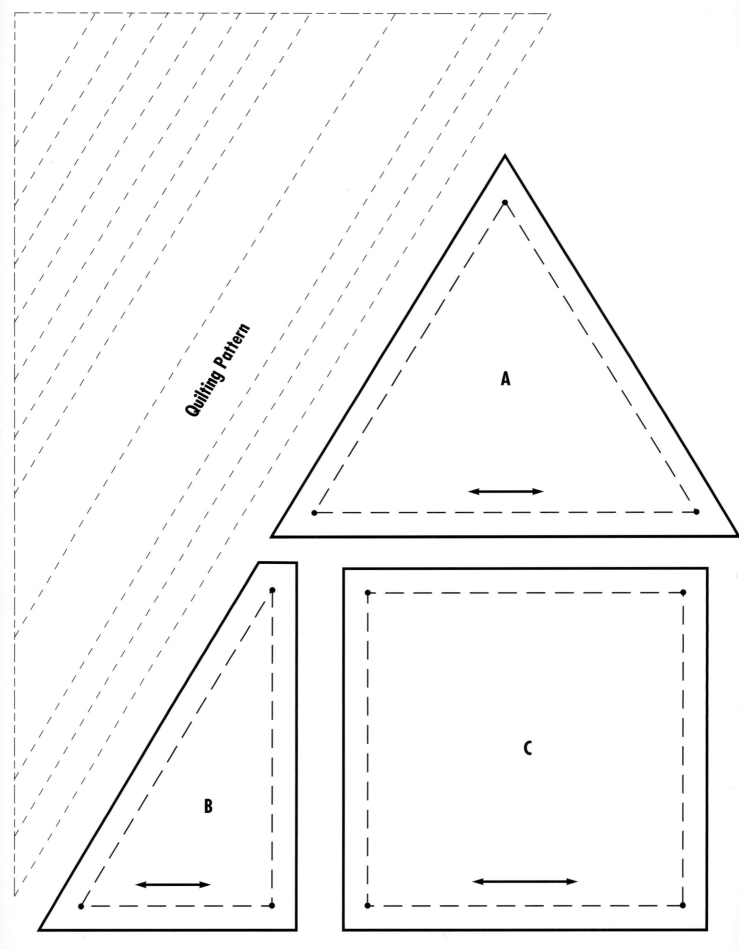

Quilting Pattern

A

B

C

devil on the run

Quilt by Nancy Wagner Graves of Manhattan, Kansas

Curved seams aren't *sew* difficult. A little practice will leave you wondering what the fuss was about. The basic unit of this patchwork is a curve-seamed two-patch that appears in traditional Drunkard's Path designs. A Devil's Puzzle variation inspired the name of this quilt, hand-pieced on-the-go by Nancy Graves. Contrasting piping, sewn in with the binding, adds a nice finishing touch.

Finished Size
Quilt: 84" x 102"
Blocks: 20 blocks, 18" x 18"
This quilt fits a full-size or a queen-size bed. See Size Variations (page 42) for other size requirements.

Materials
952 (3½") scrap squares
6¾ yards background fabric
⅞ yard binding fabric
3⅛ yards 90"-wide backing fabric
10¾ yards ⅛"-diameter cording (optional)
90" x 108" precut batting
⅛"-diameter hole punch

Devil's Puzzle Block—Make 20.

Unit 1—Make 360.

Unit 2—Make 552.

Making Blocks

Make templates of patterns X, Y, and Z on page 44. Mark matching dots on templates as shown on patterns X and Y. Use a ⅛"-diameter hole punch to punch dots in each template. *Note:* There are excellent ready-made templates available for Drunkard's Path patchwork. Look for templates at your quilt shop or in mail-order catalogs (see page 160).

1. From scraps, cut 360 of X, 552 of Y, and 40 Z squares. Mark dots on wrong side of each X and Y piece.

2. Set aside ⅓ yard of background fabric for piping. From remaining background fabric, cut 552 of X and 360 of Y. Mark all pieces as before.

3. Referring to PinPoints on page 41, choose desired method for sewing curved seam. Make 360 of Unit 1 as shown, using scrap Xs and background Ys. Then make 552 of Unit 2, using background Xs and scrap Ys.

4. For each block, select 16 of Unit 1 and 20 of Unit 2. Arrange units in six horizontal rows (**Block Assembly Diagram**). When satisfied with

placement, join units in each row. Then join rows to complete block. Make 20 blocks.

5. For partial block, select two of Unit 1, eight of Unit 2, and two Z squares. Arrange units in two horizontal rows (**Partial Block Diagram**). Join units in each row; then join rows to complete partial block. Make 18 partial blocks.

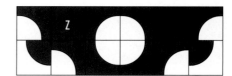

Partial Block—Make 18.

6. For corner block, select one of Unit 1, two of Unit 2, and one Z square. Join units in two rows as shown (**Corner Block Diagram**); then join rows to complete corner block. Make four corner blocks.

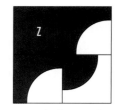

Corner Block—Make 4.

Block Assembly Diagram

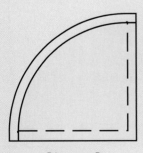

pinpoints

Piecing a Curved Seam

Piecing curves doesn't have to be difficult. It just requires a little extra care to ensure a smooth, accurate seam. Try making a few practice units, using the methods described below, to see which technique you like best.

Machine Piecing

1. On each Y piece, make small clips between dots as shown on pattern. Be careful not to cut into seam line. Clips let seam allowance spread so curved edges will match for piecing.
2. Match one X and one Y, right sides facing. Pin curved edges together, matching dots (**Diagram A**). Let Y piece gather as necessary, but make it as smooth as possible at curved edge.
3. With Y piece on top, machine-stitch curved seam. Start at one end and carefully stitch around curve, smoothing creases away from seam as you sew. Remove each pin before you stitch over it.
4. Press seam allowance toward Y (**Diagram B**). If necessary, a hot iron can work out tiny puckers in the seam.

Hand Piecing

1. Clip and pin pieces as described for machine piecing.
2. Make a knot in end of sewing thread. Bring up needle to start stitching at first dot.
3. Making a small running stitch, carefully sew from dot to dot. Remove pins as you go.
4. At last dot, knot off thread.
5. Press seam allowance toward Y (**Diagram B**).

Appliqué

This method takes more time but produces a smooth, perfect curve on each seam.

1. Make a pressing template for piece X. Use Templar (a heat-resistant, translucent nylon sheet available at quilting shops or from mail-order sources) or a lightweight aluminum such as the bottom of a disposable pie pan. (This is a good excuse to buy and eat a yummy ready-to-bake pie!) Cut pressing template so that it includes seam allowances on straight edges but *does not* include seam allowance along curve (**Diagram C**).
2. Place fabric piece X facedown on ironing board. Spray curved edge with water or spray starch. Place pressing template on fabric, aligning straight edges (**Diagram D**). Use tip of iron to press curved seam allowance back over template edge. (If using aluminum template, keep your fingers away from the iron—metal will become hot at pressed edge.) When seam allowance is dry, remove template.
3. Aligning straight edges, pin X to Y (**Diagram E**).
4. Using thread that matches X, stitch curved edge with a machine topstitch (**Diagram F**) or hand-blind-stitch (**Diagram G**).

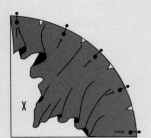

Diagram A

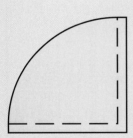

Diagram B

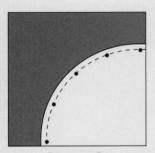

Diagram C

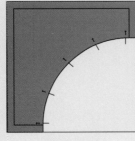

Diagram D

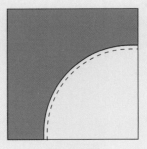

Diagram E

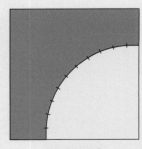

Diagram F

Diagram G

Row 1—Make 2.

Row 2—Make 5.

Row Assembly Diagram

Quilt Assembly

1. For Row 1, join two corner blocks and four partial blocks as shown **(Row Assembly Diagram)**. Make two of Row 1.
2. For Row 2, join four blocks and two partial blocks as shown. Make five of Row 2.
3. Referring to photo on page 43, join five of Row 2. Then join Row 1s to top and bottom edges of quilt as shown.

Quilting and Finishing

1. Mark quilting design on quilt top as desired. Quilt shown is outline-quilted, with a curved-edge square quilted in center of each four-patch of background fabric **(Quilting Pattern)**.
2. Layer backing, batting, and quilt top. Baste. Quilt as desired.
3. From remaining background fabric, cut ten 1"-wide crossgrain strips. Sew strips end-to-end to make a continuous strip for piping. Cover cording with strip, leaving a seam allowance of approximately ⅜".
4. Matching raw edges, pin piping around outside edge of quilt top. Clip piping seam allowance at quilt corners.
5. Make 10¾ yards of bias or straight-grain binding. See page 156 for instructions on making and applying binding. Piping is sewn into binding seam as you go.

Size Variations

	Crib	Twin	King
Finished Size	42" x 42"	66" x 84"	102" x 102"
Number of			
Blocks	4	12	25
Partial Blocks	8	14	20
Corner Blocks	4	4	4
Blocks Set	2 x 2	3 x 4	5 x 5
Yardage Required			
Scrap squares	256	616	1,156
Background fabric	2¼ yards	5½ yards	9¾ yards
Binding fabric	⅝ yard	⅞ yard	1 yard
Backing fabric	1⅜ yards	2⅛ yards (90" wide)	3⅛ yards (120" wide)

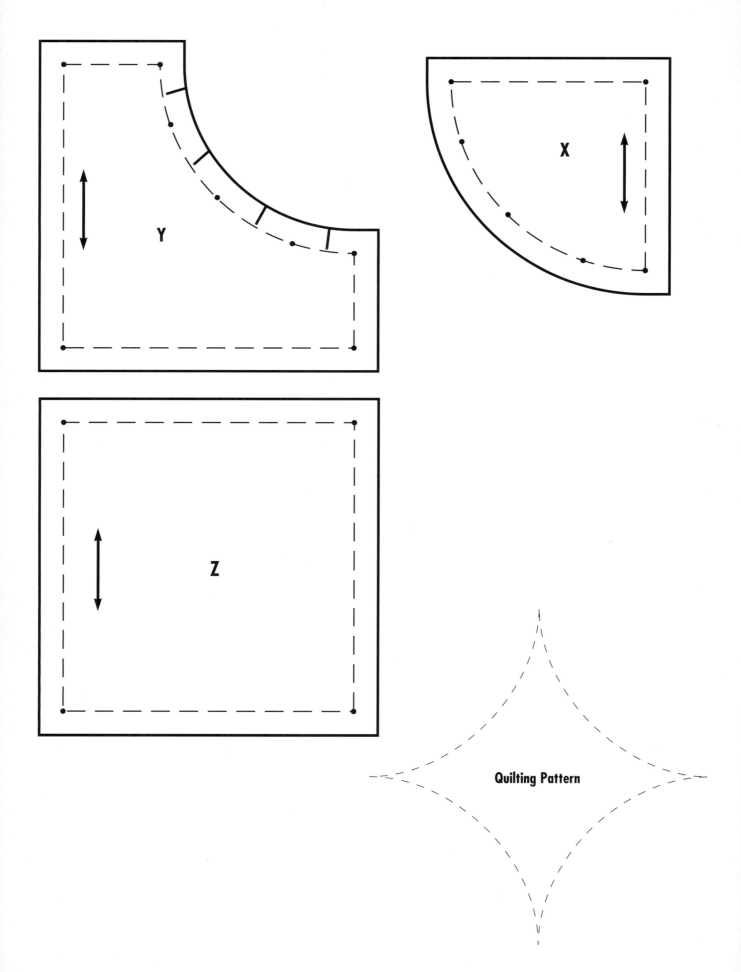

Quilting Pattern

bedding down

Winter is serious business in Alaska, where quilts must be especially warm and cozy. A cheerful assortment of handsome plaid fabrics makes Kristina Bell's quilt a classic example that warms the soul as well as hands and feet. What looks like an allover pattern is really 20 blocks of a design called Barrister's Block.

Finished Size

Quilt: 74" x 90"
Blocks: 20 blocks, 16" x 16"
This quilt fits a twin-size or full-size bed. See Size Variations (page 47) for other size requirements.

Materials

40 (6⅞") squares light/medium plaid fabrics
40 (6⅞") squares medium/dark plaid fabrics
20 (9½" x 18") white-on-white scraps or 1⅝ yards of one fabric
20 (7" x 18") pieces of dark solid fabrics
½ yard fabric for inner border
2½ yards fabric for outer border
⅞ yard binding fabric
5½ yards backing fabric
81" x 96" precut batting

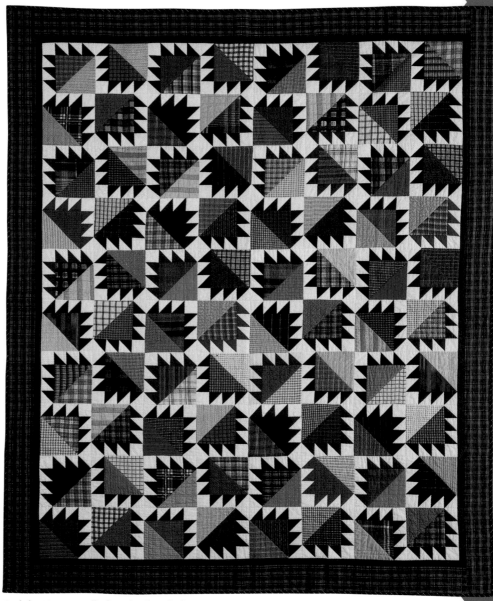

Quilt by Kristina Bell of Fairbanks, Alaska

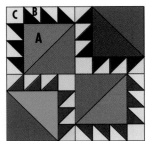

Barrister's Block — Make 20.

Making Blocks

Instructions are for rotary cutting and quick piecing. Before cutting, read block instructions and decide whether you prefer quick piecing or traditional piecing. For traditional cutting, use patterns on page 47.

The Barrister's Block has four quadrants, each a different combination of fabrics.

1. On wrong side of a light/medium plaid square, draw a diagonal line from corner to corner. Match marked square with a dark fabric, right sides facing. Sewing a ¼" seam allowance, stitch through both layers on *both sides* of line **(Diagram A)**.

2. Cut on drawn line to get two triangle-squares. Make a total of 80 triangle-squares. Press seam allowances toward darker fabrics.

3. From each white-on-white fabric, cut a 2½" x 18" strip. From this, cut four 2½" C squares. Set squares aside.

4. On wrong side of each 7" x 18" piece of white-on-white fabric, draw a 2-square by 6-square grid of 2⅞" squares **(Diagram B)**. Mark diagonal lines through centers of squares as shown.

5. Match each marked piece with a solid fabric, right sides facing. Stitch on both sides of diagonal lines, pivoting at each grid corners as shown. (Red line on diagram shows continuous stitching line; blue line indicates second stitching line.) Press stitching. Cut on all drawn lines to get 24 triangle-squares from each grid. Press seam allowances toward dark fabric.

6. Sort out 80 sets of small triangle-squares, six for each quadrant. Match each set with a plaid triangle-square and one C square.

7. Join small triangle-squares in two rows of three squares each, sewing light side of one square to dark side of next square **(Diagram C)**. Press seams toward dark fabric.

8. Positioning plaid triangle-square with dark side on the left as shown, sew one row of small triangle-squares to right side of large square. Sew C square to dark end of remaining row; then sew this row to top of plaid square as shown. In this manner, make 80 units.

9. Select four units for each block. Referring to block diagram for positioning, join units in pairs; then join pairs to complete block. Make 20 blocks.

Quilt Assembly

1. Lay out blocks in five horizontal rows with four blocks in each row **(Row Assembly Diagram)**. Rearrange blocks as desired to achieve a pleasing balance of color and value.

2. When satisfied with placement, join blocks in each row.

3. Join rows as shown in photo.

Borders

1. For inner border, cut eight 1½"-wide crosswise strips. Join two strips end-to-end to make each border.

2. Referring to page 150, measure quilt from top to bottom and trim side borders to match length. Sew borders to quilt sides.

3. Measure quilt from side to side and trim remaining borders to match quilt width. Sew borders to top and bottom edges of quilt.

4. For outer border, cut four 4½"-wide lengthwise strips. Measure quilt, trim, and sew outer borders as for inner border.

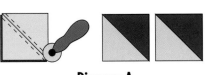

Diagram A

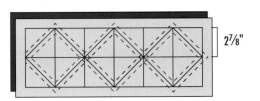

2⅞"

Diagram B

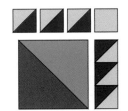

Diagram C

Row Assembly Diagram

Quilting and Finishing

1. Mark quilting design on quilt top as desired. On quilt shown, quilting follows lines in plaid fabrics.
2. Cut backing into two equal lengths. Cut one piece in half lengthwise. Sew a narrow panel to each side of wide piece to assemble backing.
3. Layer backing, batting, and quilt top. Backing seams will parallel top and bottom edges of quilt. Baste. Quilt as desired.
4. Make 9½ yards of bias or straight-grain binding. See page 156 for instructions on making and applying binding.

Size Variations

	Queen	King
Finished Size	90" x 90"	106" x 106"
Number of Blocks	25	36
Blocks Set	5 x 5	6 x 6
Yardage Required		
Light/medium squares	50	72
Medium/dark squares	50	72
White-on-white fabrics	25 or 2 yards	36 or 2½ yards
Solid fabrics	25	36
Inner border fabric	½ yard	⅝ yard
Outer border fabric	2¾ yards	3⅛ yards
Binding fabric	⅞ yard	1 yard
Backing fabric	8¼ yards	9⅜ yards

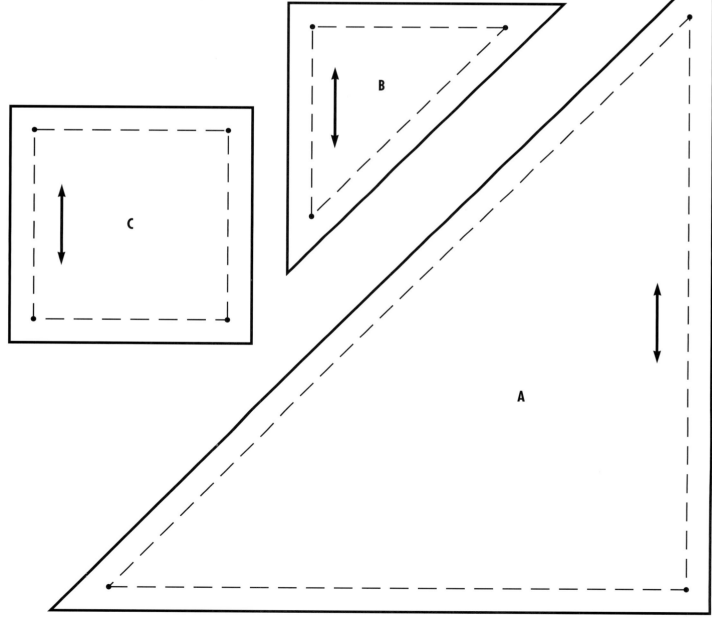

cups & saucers

Quilt by Sissy Graves Towers of Rainbow City, Alabama

When sorting scraps by color, most fabric lovers find one color group stacked higher than others. Use this hidden tendency to combine your favorite-colored fabrics with simple patchwork and appliqué to create a collection of saucy teacups based on a popular 1930s pattern.

Finished Size

Quilt: 74½" x 98"
Blocks: 77 blocks, 6¾" x 7"
This quilt fits a full-size bed.
See Size Variations (page 49)
for other size requirements.

Materials

77 (5" x 7") scraps
3½ yards muslin
3¾ yards blue setting fabric
   (includes binding)
5¾ yards backing fabric
81" x 96" precut batting

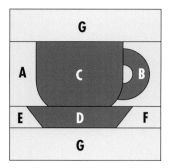

Cups and Saucers Block—Make 77.

Making Blocks

Make templates of patterns on page 50. Pieces A and G can be rotary-cut, if desired. See page 144 for tips on cutting pieces for appliqué and patchwork with templates.

1. From muslin, cut 13 (3½"-wide) cross-grain strips and 15 (1½"-wide) strips. From these, cut 77 (3½" x 7¼") A pieces and 77 *each* of E and F. From remaining muslin, cut 154 (2" x 7¼") Gs.
2. From each scrap fabric, cut one D; then cut one each of appliqué pieces B and C, adding seam allowances. Prepare pieces for appliqué by turning under curved edges. Do not turn under straight edges, which will be overlapped or finished in the seams.
3. Position B and C on A, aligning straight edges of A and C. Place curve of handle (B) about ¾" from right edge of A. Cup overlaps ends of handle. When satisfied with position, appliqué B and C in place (**Block Assembly Diagram**).

Size Variations

	Twin	Queen	King
Finished Size	61" x 91"	88" x 98"	95" x 105"
Number of Blocks	59	91	105
Number of Set Blocks	58	91	105
Blocks Set	9 x 13	13 x 14	14 x 15
Yardage Required			
5" x 7" scraps	59	91	105
Muslin	2½ yards	4 yards	4⅝ yards
Setting fabric	2⅞ yards	4 yards	4¾ yards
Backing fabric	5½ yards	2⅝ yards (108" wide)	3⅛ yards (108" wide)

4. Sew E and F to D as shown to complete saucer section. Press seam allowances toward D.
5. Join saucer section to bottom of teacup section.
6. Sew Gs to top and bottom of block.
7. Make 77 blocks.

Quilt Assembly

1. From blue fabric, cut 77 (7¼" x 7½") pieces for setting blocks.
2. For Row 1, lay out six blocks and five setting blocks in a row, alternating blocks as shown (**Row Assembly Diagram**). For Row 2, lay out five blocks and six setting blocks as shown.
3. Referring to photo, lay out blocks in 14 rows, alternating rows 1 and 2. Arrange blocks to achieve a nice balance of color and value.

When satisfied with placement, join blocks in each row.
4. Referring to photo, join rows.

Quilting and Finishing

1. Mark quilting design on quilt top as desired. On quilt shown, patchwork is outline-quilted and a purchased stencil design is quilted in each setting block.
2. Divide backing into two equal lengths. Cut one piece in half lengthwise. Join narrow panels to sides of wide piece to assemble backing.
3. Layer backing, batting, and quilt top. Baste. Quilt as desired.
4. Make 10 yards of bias or straight-grain binding. See page 156 for instructions on making and applying binding.

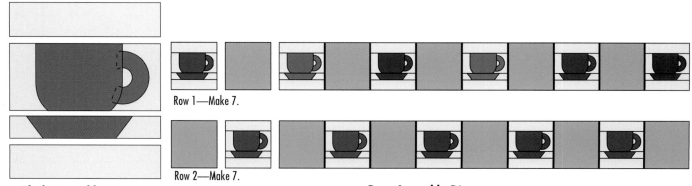

Block Assembly Diagram

Row 1—Make 7.

Row 2—Make 7.

Row Assembly Diagram

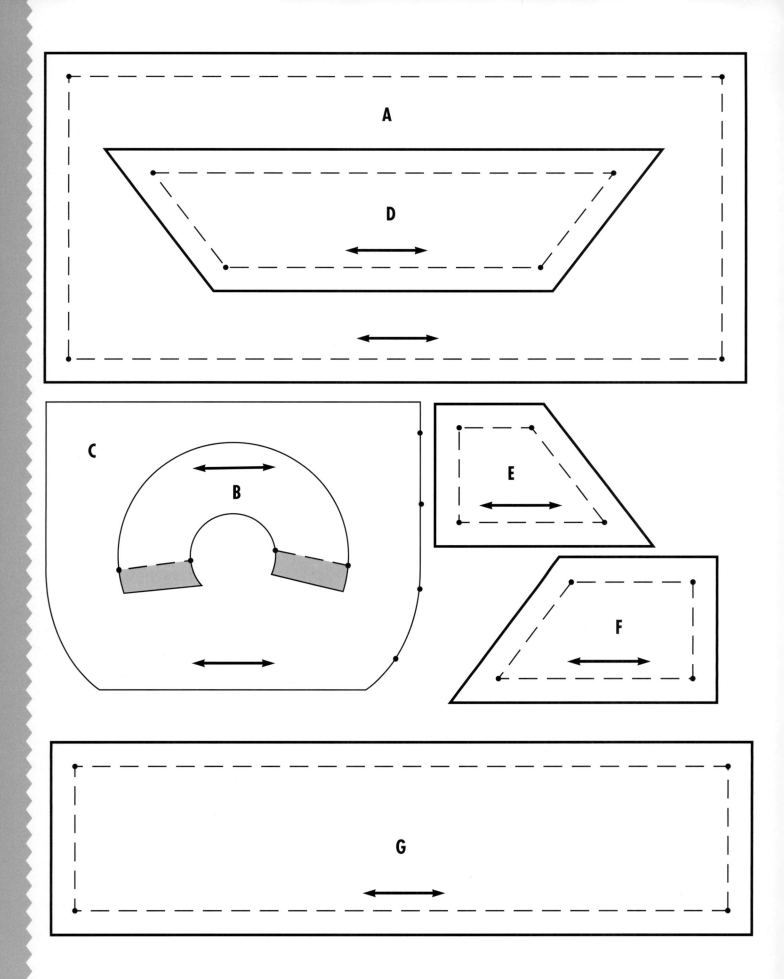

maple street rag

Don't let a riot of fabrics make you think this quilt is hard to sew—it's made of simple Maple Leaf blocks. For the windswept leaves, Karen Kratz-Miller uses a host of fabrics, mostly plaids, in warm autumn colors of gold, orange, and hot pink, with just a bit of summer's green. Stars on the black background fabrics evoke a night sky, while splashes of blue herald the coming day. For a winter's tale of Maple Street, see Karen's cool version of this quilt on pages 54 and 55.

Finished Size

Quilt: 65" x 85"
Blocks: 48 blocks, 10" x 10"
This quilt fits a twin-size bed.
See Size Variations (page 53)
for other size requirements.

Materials

48 fat eighths (9" x 22") pieces
    of autumn-colored fabrics or
    equivalent scraps
48 fat eighths (9" x 22") of
    black and blue fabrics or
    equivalent scraps
⅞ yard binding fabric
2 yards 90"-wide backing fabric
72" x 90" precut batting

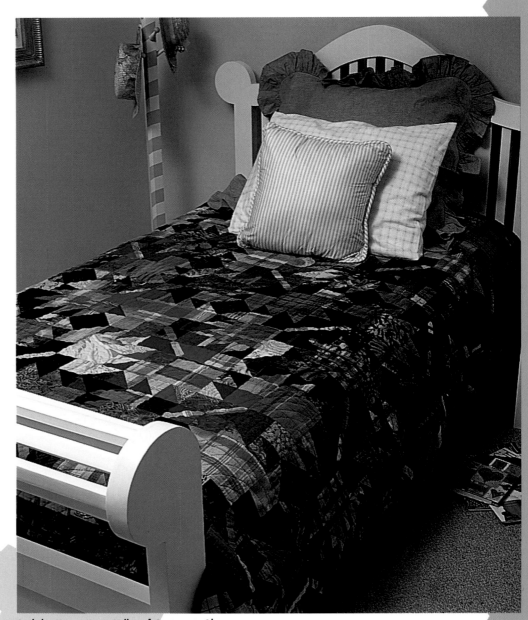

Quilt by Karen Kratz-Miller of Cincinnati, Ohio

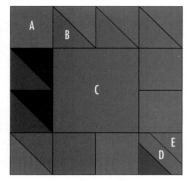

Maple Leaf Block—Make 48.

Making Blocks

Instructions are for rotary cutting and quick piecing. See page 146 for directions on quick-pieced triangle-squares and diagonal-corner technique. For traditional cutting, use patterns on page 56.

1. From each colored fabric, cut a 4½" x 11" piece for B triangle-squares, one 5½" C square, and three 3" squares for A and D.
2. From each black or blue fabric, cut a 4½" x 11" piece for B triangle-squares, three 3" A squares, and two 2¼" squares for Es. Save remaining fabric for border squares.
3. On wrong side of each 4½" x 11" light fabric, mark a three-square grid of 3⅜" squares (Diagram A). Mark diagonal lines through centers of squares as shown.

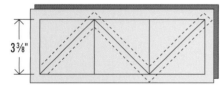

Diagram A

4. Match one light fabric to one dark fabric, right sides together. Stitch on both sides of diagonal lines, pivoting at corners as shown. Press stitching.
5. Cut on all drawn lines to get six triangle-squares. Press seam allowances toward dark fabric.

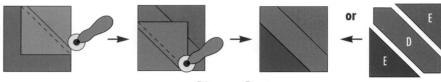

Diagram B

6. Use diagonal-corner technique to make stem square. Sew 2¼" dark square to top right corner of 3" square of light fabric as shown (Diagram B). Trim seam allowance and press corner to right side. Repeat with another 2¼" dark square in bottom left corner as shown. (For traditional piecing, sew E triangles to opposite sides of D piece as shown.)
7. For each block, select six triangle-squares, one C square, two light A squares, three dark A squares, and one D/E stem square. Choose units of the same fabrics or varied fabrics, as desired. Arrange squares in three rows as shown (Block Assembly Diagram). Join squares in rows; then join rows to complete block.
8. Make 48 Maple Leaf blocks.

Quilt Assembly

1. Lay out blocks in eight horizontal rows with six blocks in each row. In rows 1, 3, 5, and 7, block positions alternate between stem in bottom right corner and stem in top right corner (Row Assembly Diagram). In rows 2, 4, 6, and 8, stem position alternates between

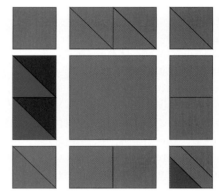

Block Assembly Diagram

bottom left corner and top left corner as shown.

2. From remaining dark fabrics, cut 116 (3") A squares. For each border unit, join four A squares in a row. Make 16 units. Place a unit at both ends of each row as shown.
3. Rearrange blocks and border units as desired to achieve a pleasing balance of color and value. When satisfied with placement, join blocks and border units in each row.
4. Join rows as shown in photo on page 53.
5. For top and bottom borders, assemble two rows with 26 A squares in each row. Sew rows to top and bottom edges of quilt.

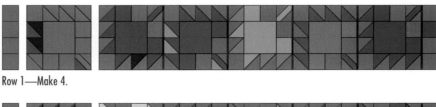

Row 1—Make 4.

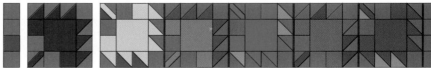

Row 2—Make 4.

Row Assembly Diagram

Quilting and Finishing

1. Mark quilting design on quilt top as desired. Quilt shown is quilted in an allover pattern of concentric arcs that is sometimes called the Baptist Fan.

2. Layer backing, batting, and quilt top. Baste. Quilt as desired.

3. Make 8⅝ yards of bias or straight-grain binding. See page 156 for instructions on making and applying binding.

Size Variations

	Full	Queen	King
Finished Size	75" x 95"	85" x 95"	95" x 95"
Number of Blocks	63	72	81
Blocks Set	7 x 9	8 x 9	9 x 9
Number of Border Squares	132	140	148

Yardage Required

Light fat eighths	63	72	81
Dark fat eighths	63	72	81
Binding fabric	⅞ yard	⅞ yard	1 yard
108"-wide backing fabric	2⅜ yards	2⅝ yards	3 yards

maple street blues

Quilt by Karen Kratz-Miller of Cincinnati, Ohio

all seasons have unique beauty, and Karen Kratz-Miller catches their colors in a series of Maple Street quilts. Compare this frosty version with the warmth of *Maple Street Rag* (page 53). Here, placement of white and black background fabrics tells a winter's tale of a snowy night on Maple Street. Cutting big, graphic prints into small squares makes the background shimmer like swirling snowflakes.

Finished Size

Quilt: 55" x 55"
Blocks: 25 blocks, 10" x 10"

Materials

48 fat eighths (9" x 22" pieces) of blue fabrics or equivalent scraps
5 fat eighths (9" x 22" pieces) of black-on-white prints
10 fat eighths (9" x 22" pieces) of black-and-white prints
5 fat eighths (9" x 22" pieces) of white-on-black prints
½ yard striped binding fabric
1¾ yards backing fabric
60" x 60" batting

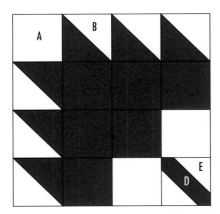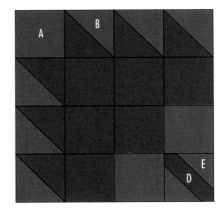

Maple Leaf Block—Make 25.

Making Blocks

This Maple Leaf block is made in the same manner as described on page 52 except that four A squares replace square C.

1. From each blue fabric, cut one 4½" x 11" piece for B triangle-squares and seven 3" squares for A and D.
2. From each background fabric, cut a 4½" x 11" piece for B triangle-squares, three 3" A squares, and two 2¼" squares for E. Save remaining fabric for border squares.
3. Follow instructions on page 52 to make triangle-squares and stem squares. Assemble squares as shown **(Block Assembly Diagram)**. Make 25 blocks, changing background colors from mostly white to mostly black.

Block Assembly Diagram

Quilt Assembly

1. From remaining background fabric, cut 84 (3") A squares for border. Join 22 white squares and 22 black squares for top and bottom borders. Join remaining squares in four-square units as described on page 52, making each unit from similar fabrics as pictured.
2. Referring to photo on page 54, make five rows of five blocks each as described on page 52. Add border units to rows. Join rows.
3. Join top and bottom borders to quilt.

Quilting and Finishing

1. Mark quilting design on quilt top as desired. Quilt shown is machine-quilted with undulating lines of "wind."
2. Divide backing into two equal lengths. Cut one piece in half lengthwise. Join a narrow panel to each side of wide piece to assemble backing.
3. Layer backing, batting, and quilt top. Backing seams will parallel top and bottom edges of quilt. Baste. Quilt as desired.
4. Make 6⅜ yards of straight-grain binding. See page 156 for instructions on making and applying binding.

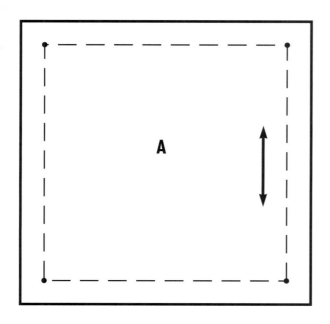

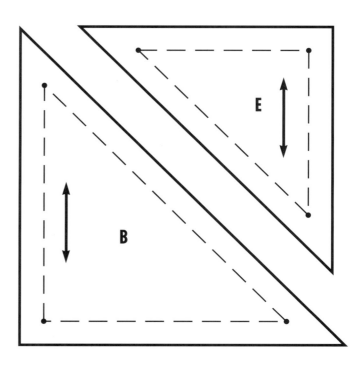

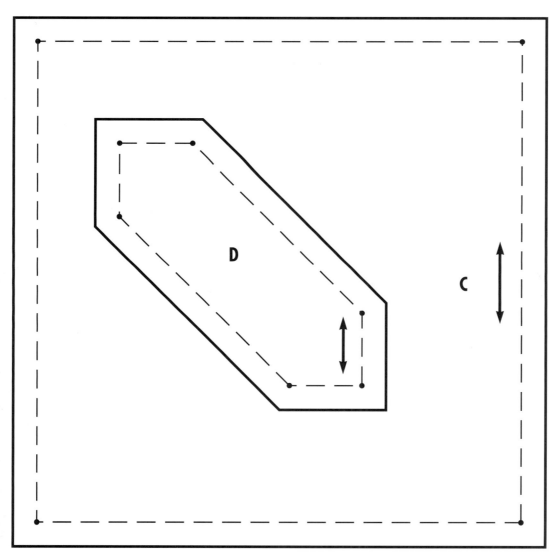

baskets of Liberty

Marvelous print fabrics give these baskets real flower power. The fabrics are from Liberty of London (a manufacturer of fine-quality cotton fabrics), hence the name Beverly Leasure gives her quilt. Pick a bouquet of favorite prints for a fabulously floral quilt all your own.

Finished Size

Quilt: 66" x 87"
Blocks: 35 blocks, 9" x 9"
This quilt fits a twin-size bed. Because of the pieced border, size variations are not recommended for this quilt.

Materials

35 fat eighths (9" x 22" pieces) or equivalent scraps
1¼ yards light print fabric for sashing squares, pieced border
2 yards muslin
2⅝ yards dark print fabric
5½ yards backing fabric
72" x 90" precut batting

Making Blocks

Instructions are for rotary cutting. For traditional cutting, use patterns on page 60.

1. From each print fabric, cut three 4¼" squares and four 2⅜" squares. (Set aside remaining print fabric for borders.) Cut larger squares in quarters diagonally to get 12 A triangles. Cut smaller squares in half diagonally to get eight B triangles. Divide triangles into two sets, one for each of two blocks.

Quilt by Beverly A. Leasure of Dunedin, Florida

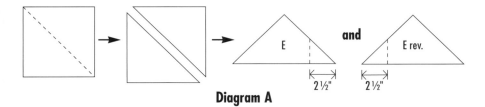

Diagram A

2. From muslin, cut nine 7¼" squares and 35 (5⅜") squares. Cut larger squares in quarters diagonally to get 35 C triangles (and one extra). Cut smaller squares in half diagonally to get 70 D triangles.

3. From remaining muslin, cut 35 (5⅜") squares. Cut squares in half diagonally, just as you did for D triangles. For E pieces, trim 2½" from longest edge (hypotenuse) as shown **(Diagram A)**. Be sure to cut 35 triangles on the right side (E) and 35 triangles on the left side (E reversed).

4. For each block, select two sets of triangles, generally one light-valued fabric and another of medium or dark value. Also select one C triangle, two D triangles, and one each of E and E reversed.

5. Join B triangles in four light-dark pairs as shown **(Block Assembly Diagram)**. To make basket handle, join two pairs to make two diagonal rows as shown. Sew rows to short sides of C triangle. Press seam allowances toward C.

6. Sew a light A triangle to top of handle section. Press seam allowance toward A.

7. Sew Ds to sides of unit as shown to complete top half of block.

8. For bottom half, join light and dark A triangles in three rows as shown. Join rows to make a large triangle.

9. Sew light A triangles to ends of E and E reversed as shown. Sew units to sides of large triangle to complete bottom half of block.

10. Join halves to complete block.

11. Make 35 blocks in this manner.

Quilt Assembly

1. From dark print fabric, cut a 20"-wide lengthwise strip for borders. From remainder, cut 58 (2¼" x 9½") strips for sashing.

2. From light print fabric, cut 24 (2¼") squares for sashing.

3. Lay out blocks in seven horizontal rows of five blocks each. Join blocks in each row, sewing a sashing strip between blocks as shown **(Row Assembly Diagram)**.

4. For sashing row, join five sashing strips and four squares as shown. Press seam allowances toward sashing. Make six sashing rows.

5. Join rows as shown in photo, alternating block rows and sashing rows.

Borders

1. For inner border, cut four 3"-wide lengthwise strips.

2. Referring to page 150, measure quilt from top to bottom and trim two borders to match length. Sew borders to quilt sides.

3. Measure quilt from side to side and trim remaining borders to match quilt width. Sew borders to top and bottom edges of quilt.

4. See page 146 to decide whether you prefer diagonal-corner quick-piecing technique or traditional piecing for middle border. For quick piecing, cut 376 (2") squares from remaining light print fabric and 94 (3½") squares from print scraps, cutting two or three squares from each fabric. For traditional cutting, use templates B and G.

5. Use diagonal-corner technique to sew four light corners on each G square **(Diagram B)**. Or sew B triangles to G square traditionally as shown. Assembled unit should be 3½" square. Make 94 units.

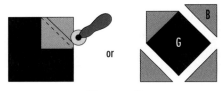

Diagram B

6. For each side border, join 26 units in a row. Sew borders to quilt sides, easing quilt to fit as needed.

Block Assembly Diagram

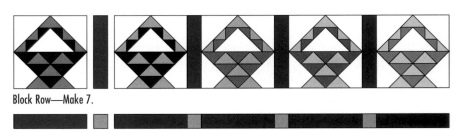

Block Row—Make 7.

Sashing Row—Make 6.

Row Assembly Diagram

7. Join 21 units in each row for top and bottom borders. Sew borders to top and bottom edges of quilt.

8. For outer border, cut four 2"-wide lengthwise strips from remaining dark print fabric. Measure quilt; then trim and sew borders to quilt as for inner border.

Quilting and Finishing

1. Mark quilting design on quilt top as desired. Quilt shown has outline quilting and cross-hatching in D triangles as shown on pattern. See Pattern C for feather motif quilted in those triangles.

2. For prairie points, cut 202 (2¾") H squares from remaining scraps. See PinPoints below to add prairie point edging. If prairie points are not desired, see page 156 for tips on binding quilt traditionally when quilting is complete.

3. Divide backing into two equal lengths. Cut one piece in half lengthwise. Join a narrow panel to each side of wide piece to assemble backing.

4. Layer backing, batting, and quilt top. Baste. Quilt as desired.

5. Blindstitch backing as described in PinPoints.

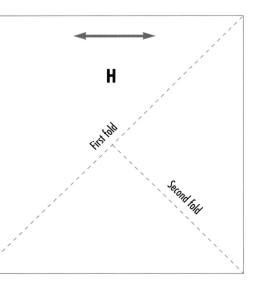

H

First fold

Second fold

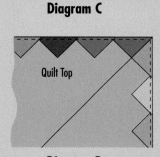

pinpoints

Prairie Point Edging

Adding an edging of prairie points is a popular and attractive way to finish a quilt. Making the points is as simple as folding a square.

This type of edging does not use standard binding. Instead, the backing edges are turned under and blindstitched in place by hand. This may be a less sturdy finish than a machine-stitched binding, so reserve prairie point edgings for quilts that will not see a lot of wear.

To be able to turn the backing under, be sure quilting stops at least ½" from edge of quilt top.

1. Fold each fabric square in half diagonally, wrong sides together, (Diagram A). Press.

2. Fold each triangle in half again to make a smaller triangle (Diagram B). Press.

3. Arrange prairie points on right side of quilt, aligning raw edges of triangles and quilt top. Triangles will overlap, with each one fitting between the folds of its neighbor (Diagram C). Space prairie points evenly along each side. For *Baskets of Liberty,* position 57 points on each side and 44 points at top and bottom edges.

4. When satisfied with placement of prairie points, topstitch in place ¼" from raw edge (Diagram D).

5. Layer quilt with batting and backing. Quilt as desired.

6. Trim backing fabric even with quilt top. Trim batting ¼" shorter than quilt top on all sides.

7. Turn points so they face out from quilt top, turning under raw edge of quilt top. Press lightly.

8. Turn under ¼" on all sides of backing fabric. Blindstitch folded edge of backing to back of prairie point edging (Diagram E).

Fold.

Fold.

Diagram A   **Diagram B**

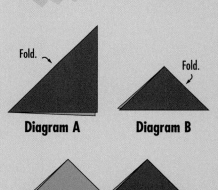

Diagram C

Quilt Top

Diagram D

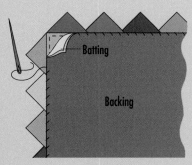

Batting

Backing

Diagram E

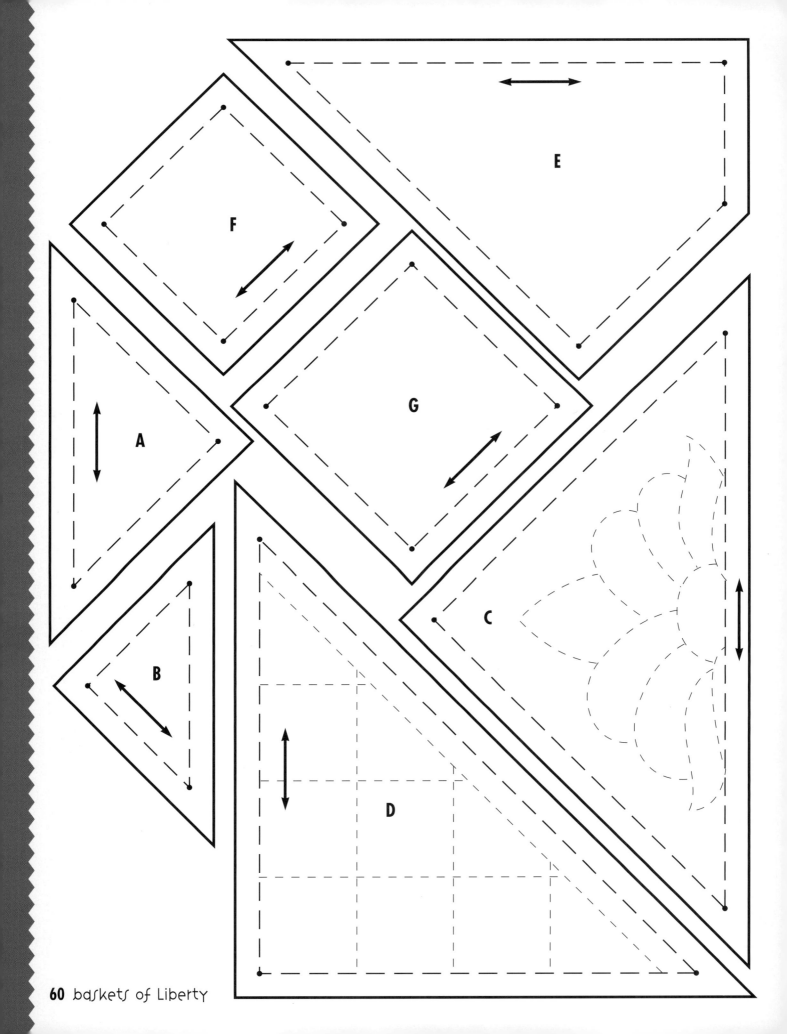

F

E

A

G

B

C

D

spider web

Red stars accent this web of Flying Geese patchwork. Wild Goose Chase blocks and sashing place scrap fabrics against a neutral background. Choose traditional piecing or quick-piecing techniques to make the geese. Marion Watchinski's quilt is patterned after one made by her husband's great-grandmother at the turn of the century.

Finished Size

Quilt: 84" x 93"
Blocks: 9 blocks, 16" x 16"
 12 half-blocks, 8½" x 16"
This quilt fits a full-size or queen-size bed. See Size Variations (page 63) for other size requirements.

Materials

768 (2⅛") scrap squares*
7½ yards muslin
1¾ yards red fabric
7¾ yards backing fabric
90" x 108" precut batting

*Note: Scraps listed are for traditional piecing. See options on page 62 for quick-piecing requirements.

Quilt by Marion Roach Watchinski of Overland Park, Kansas

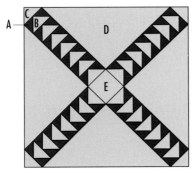

Wild Goose Chase Block—Make 9.

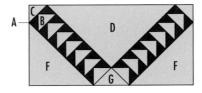

Half-Block—Make 12.

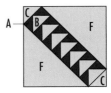

Quarter-Block—Make 4.

Cutting

Before cutting, read block piecing instructions and decide whether you prefer the diagonal-corner technique or traditional piecing for flying geese. Instructions are for rotary cutting. For traditional cutting, use patterns on page 66 to make templates.

From scraps, cut:
• 1,536 (1¾") squares to make geese with diagonal-corner technique or 768 (2⅛") squares for traditional piecing. Cut 2⅛" squares in half diagonally to get 1,536 A triangles.

From muslin, cut:
• 2 (5½" x 86") and 2 (3½" x 86") lengthwise strips for outer border.
• 4 (2¼" x 80") lengthwise strips for inner border.
• 4 (9" x 15½") pieces for triangle-squares.
• 12 (13¾") squares. Cut each square in quarters diagonally to get 48 D triangles.
• 18 (7⅛") squares. Cut each square in half diagonally to get 36 F triangles.
• 3 (4¾") squares. Cut each square in quarters diagonally to get 12 G triangles.

• 720 (1¾" x 3") pieces to make geese with diagonal-corner technique or 180 (3¾") squares for traditional piecing. Cut 3¾" squares in quarters diagonally to get 720 B triangles for geese.
• 16 (3¾") squares. Cut squares in quarters diagonally to get 64 B triangles for sashing.
• 9 (3") E squares.
• 36 (2⅝") squares. Cut each square in half diagonally to get 72 C triangles.
• 24 (3") H squares for diagonal-corner technique or 24 (2¼") H squares for traditional piecing.

From red fabric, cut:
• 4 (9" x 15½") pieces for triangle-squares.
• 8 (1¾"-wide) cross-grain strips. From these, cut 128 I diamonds. Mark seam allowances on wrong side of each diamond.

Making Blocks

1. Referring to page 146, use the diagonal-corner technique to sew two A squares to one B rectangle **(Diagram A)**. Or sew A triangles to B triangle traditionally as shown. Make 720 flying geese. Set aside 272 geese for sashing.

2. Join seven geese in a row **(Diagram B)**. Add one C triangle to left end of row as shown. Press seam allowances toward C. Make 64 geese units.

Diagram B

3. Select four geese units, four D triangles, and one E square for each block. Sew triangles to sides of two geese units as shown **(Block Assembly Diagram)**. Press seam allowances toward triangles. Sew remaining geese units to opposite

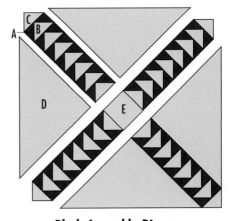

Block Assembly Diagram

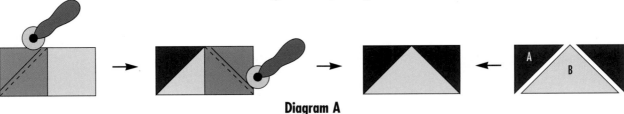

Diagram A

Sashing Unit—Make 24.

Half-Sashing Unit—Make 16.

sides of E square. Press seam allowances toward square. Join units as shown to complete block. Make nine blocks.

4. For each half-block, select two geese units, two F triangles, and one each of triangles D and G. Sew G to end of one geese unit as shown **(Half-Block Assembly Diagram)**. Sew F triangle to side of same unit. Join D and F triangles to second unit as shown. Press seam allowances toward triangles. Join halves to complete half-block. Make 12 half-blocks.

Making Sashing

1. Use diagonal-corner technique to sew four A corners on each H square **(Diagram C)**. Or sew A triangles to H square traditionally as shown.
2. Select eight geese, four I diamonds, two B triangles, and one H unit. Join four geese in a row as shown **(Sashing Assembly Diagram)**. Make two geese units.
3. Join diamonds in pairs as shown.

Referring to PinPoints on page 14, set B triangle into each pair. Sew a diamond unit to end of each geese unit.

4. Join units in a row as shown to complete sashing. Make 24 sashing units.
5. For half-sashing, join a pair of diamonds and set in a B triangle as before. Join five flying geese in a row; then sew diamond unit to one end. Make 16 half-sashing units.

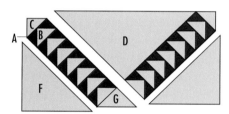

Half-Block Assembly Diagram

5. For quarter-block, sew F triangles to sides of geese unit as shown **(Quarter-Block Assembly Diagram)**. Sew C triangles to ends of geese unit. Press seam allowances toward triangles. Make four quarter-blocks.

or

Diagram C

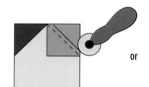

Sashing Assembly Diagram

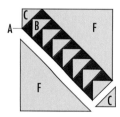

Quarter-Block Assembly Diagram

Size Variations

	Twin	King
Finished Size	65½" x 93"	102½" x 111½"
Number of		
Blocks	6	16
Half-Blocks	10	16
Quarter-Blocks	4	4
Sashing Units	17	40
Half-Sashing Units	14	20
Triangle-Squares	52	76
Blocks Set	2 x 3	4 x 4
Yardage Required		
2⅛" scrap squares	576	1,200
Muslin	6 yards	10¾ yards
Red fabric	1¾ yards	2¼ yards
Backing fabric	5⅝ yards	9½ yards

Row 1—Make 2.

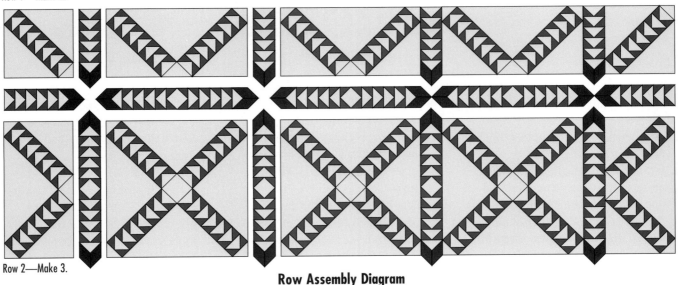

Row 2—Make 3.

Row Assembly Diagram

Quilt Assembly

Joining these rows requires careful pinning and precise sewing. See page 14 for tips on sewing set-in seams. It's a challenge, but the reward is great! Throughout assembly, refer to photo and **Row Assembly Diagram.**

1. For Row 1, join three half-blocks, two quarter-blocks, and four half-sashing units in a row as shown. Stop stitching at marked point $1/4$" from ends of diamonds. Diamond points will extend at bottom of row. Make two of Row 1.

2. For Row 2, join three blocks, two half-blocks, and four sashing units in a row as shown. Start and stop each seam at marked point on diamonds. Diamonds will extend beyond top and bottom of row. Make three of Row 2.

3. To join Row 1 to Row 2, select three sashing units and two half-sashing units. Sew long sides of sashing units to blocks, stopping at marked points on diamonds and leaving star points unstitched for now.

4. At each star center, fold back two adjacent pairs of diamonds to keep them out of the way; then

stitch a mitered seam connecting the opposite pair of diamonds **(Diagram D)**. Start stitching at block corner and sew to end of diamond points as indicated by arrow. Press seam allowance open. Stitch opposite pair in same manner. Then stitch center seam of star.

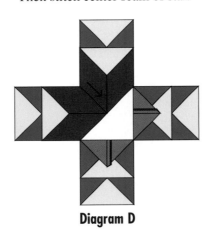

Diagram D

5. Join remaining Row 2 units in this manner. Referring to photo on page 65, end with second Row 1.

Borders

1. Referring to page 150, measure quilt and trim $2^{1/4}$"-wide muslin strips to correct length. Sew border strips to quilt edges with square corners.

2. Refer to page 148 for instructions on quick-pieced triangle-squares. On wrong side of each 9" x $15^{1/2}$" muslin piece, draw a 2-square x 4-square grid of $3^{3/8}$" squares **(Diagram E)**. Pair each muslin piece with a matching red fabric, right sides together, and stitch according to instructions on page 148.

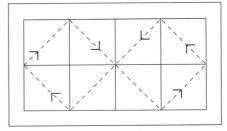

Diagram E

Start in the center of one side and follow the arrows around, pivoting at corners, to stitch the entire grid without having to remove the fabric from the sewing machine. Cut triangle-squares apart on drawn lines and press. Make 62 triangle-squares. (For traditional piecing, cut 62 J triangles from both muslin and red fabrics.)

3. Referring to photo, join 31 triangle-squares for top border. Sew border to top edge of quilt,

easing to fit as needed. Repeat for bottom border.

4. Referring to page 150, measure quilt from top to bottom and trim 3½"-wide muslin strips to correct length. Sew border strips to quilt sides. Then trim 5½"-wide muslin borders to match the quilt's width and sew these to top and bottom edges of quilt.

Quilting and Finishing

1. Mark quilting design on quilt top as desired. Quilt shown has 1"-square cross-hatching quilted in muslin areas and outline quilting inside star points.

2. Divide backing into three equal lengths. Cut one piece in half lengthwise; discard one half. Join wide panels to each side of narrow piece to assemble backing.

3. Layer backing, batting, and quilt top. Backing seams will be parallel to top and bottom edges. Baste. Quilt as desired.

4. Use remaining red fabric to make 10⅛ yards of bias or straight-grain binding. See page 156 for instructions on making and applying binding.

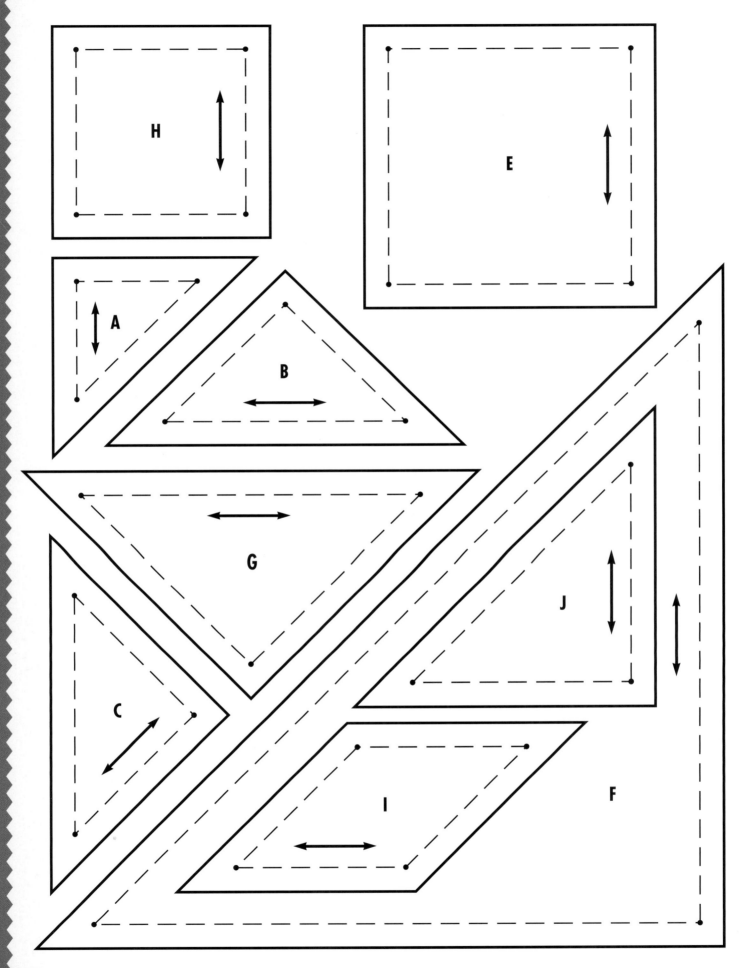

Stars in, Stars out

Seeing stars? This quilt has small stars set inside Log Cabin blocks surrounding a field of Log Cabins set inside big stars. Make a quilt with scraps of patriotic red, white, and blue, or envision a different color scheme—a masculine combination of navy, tan, and hunter green, perhaps, or dainty pastels.

Finished Size

Quilt: 60" x 84"
Blocks: 35 blocks, 12" x 12"
This quilt fits a twin-size bed.
See Size Variations (page 70) for other size requirements.

Materials

Scraps or ¼ yard each of
    8 red fabrics
Scraps or ¼ yard each of
    8 blue fabrics
Scraps or ⅛ yard each of
    5 beige/tan fabrics
1¾ yards muslin
¾ yard binding fabric
5¼ yards backing fabric
72" x 90" precut batting

Quilt by Carolyn Beam of Longmont, Colorado

Cutting

Instructions are for rotary cutting. Cut all strips cross-grain. Before cutting, read block piecing instructions and decide whether you prefer the diagonal-corner quick-piecing technique or traditional piecing for star points. For traditional cutting, use patterns on page 72.

From red fabrics, cut:
- 10 (3½") A squares.
- 80 (2") squares for diagonal corners or 40 (2⅜") squares for traditional piecing. Cut 2⅜" squares in half diagonally to get 80 B triangles.
- 7 (2") D squares.
- 56 (3½") squares for diagonal corners or 28 (3⅞") squares for traditional piecing. Cut 3⅞" squares in half diagonally to get 56 E triangles.
- 30 (1½" x 42") strips for Stars In log cabin piecing.
- 7 (1¼" x 42") strips for Stars Out log cabin piecing.

From blue fabrics, cut:
- 10 (3½") A squares.
- 80 (2") squares for diagonal corners or 40 (2⅜") squares for traditional piecing. Cut 2⅜" squares in half diagonally to get 80 B triangles.
- 8 (2") D squares.
- 64 (3½") squares for diagonal corners or 32 (3⅞") squares for traditional piecing. Cut 3⅞" squares in half diagonally to get 64 E triangles.
- 30 (1½" x 42") strips for Stars In log cabin piecing.
- 7 (1¼" x 42") strips for Stars Out log cabin piecing.

From beige/tan fabrics, cut:
- 9 (1¼" x 42") strips for Stars Out log cabin piecing.

From background fabric, cut:
- 60 (3½") A squares.
- 40 (2" x 4") pieces for diagonal corners or 10 (4¼") squares for traditional piecing. Cut 4¼" squares in quarters diagonally to get 40 C triangles.
- 40 (2") D squares.
- 60 (3½" x 6½") pieces for diagonal corners or 15 (7¼") squares for traditional piecing. Cut 7¼" squares in quarters diagonally to get 60 F triangles.

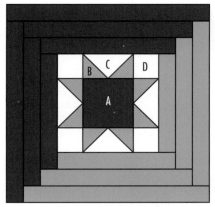

Stars In (Block 1) — Make 10.

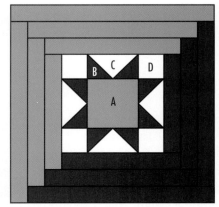

Stars In (Block 2) — Make 10.

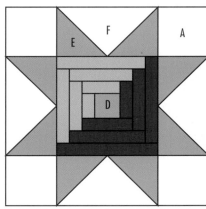

Stars Out (Block 3) — Make 8.

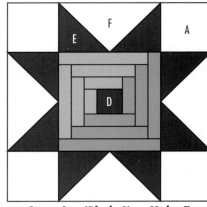

Stars Out (Block 4) — Make 7.

Stars In Blocks

There are two Stars In blocks. Placement of blue and red fabrics is reversed in blocks 1 and 2. To avoid confusion, make 10 of Block 1 (blue star points, blue logs to the right); then make 10 of Block 2 (red star points, red logs to the right).

1. Referring to page 146, use the diagonal-corner technique to sew two blue B squares to one C rectangle (**Diagram A**). Or sew B triangles to C triangle traditionally. Make four units for each block with same blue fabric for points.

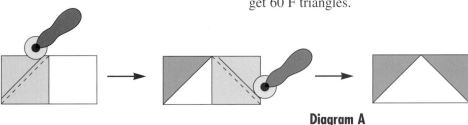

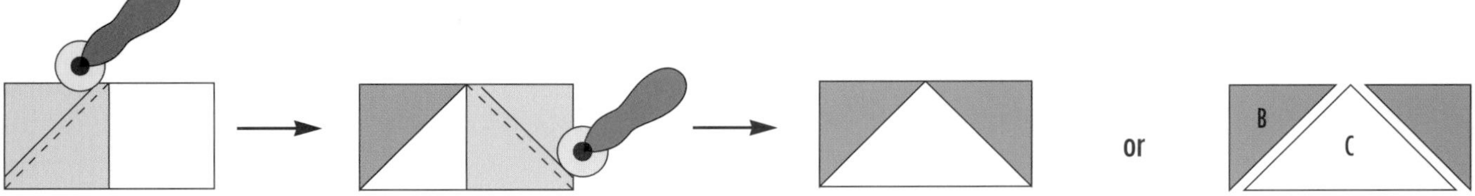

Diagram A

2. For star, select one red A square, four B/C units, and four D squares of background fabric. Join units in three rows as shown (**Diagram B**); then join rows to assemble star. Make 10 stars with red centers and blue points. Star block should measure approximately 6½" square.

3. To build a cabin around each star, select six blue strips and six red strips for logs. (Be sure to select 1½"-wide strips.) For first log, match one blue strip to right side of star block as shown (**Diagram C**) and stitch. Trim log even with bottom of star block. Press seam allowance toward log.

4. Turn block so log is at top. With right sides facing, match another blue strip to block edge and stitch (**Diagram D**). Trim new log even with block as before and press seam allowance toward log.

5. Turn unit so last log is at top. With right sides facing, match a red strip to next edge of block and stitch (**Diagram E**). Trim log even with block and press.

6. Continue adding red and blue logs in this manner until you have three logs on all sides of star block (see **Block 1 Diagram**). Always press seam allowances toward newest log. Completed block will measure approximately 12½" square.

7. Make 10 of Block 1 in this manner. Then make 10 of Block 2 in same manner, reversing positions of blue and red fabrics as shown in **Block Diagrams**.

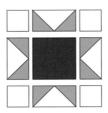

Diagram B

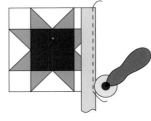

Diagram C

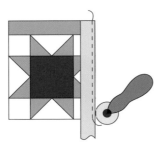

Diagram D

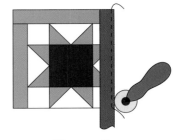

Diagram E

Stars Out Blocks

There are two Stars Out blocks, which add tan fabrics to alternating blue and red fabrics. Make eight of Block 3 (blue star points, red logs) and make seven of Block 4 (red star points, blue logs). Use 1¼"-wide strips for log cabin piecing.

1. For each Block 4, select one red D square, six blue strips, and six tan strips. Starting with tan strips, piece logs around center square as before until you have three logs on each side of the square. Pieced Log Cabin should be approximately 6½" square.

2. For star points, use diagonal-corner technique to sew two red E squares to one F rectangle, or sew E triangles to F triangle traditionally. Make four units for each block with same red fabric for points.

3. Position Log Cabin block with blue logs to right and bottom of center square. Sew E/F units to block sides as shown (**Diagram F**).

Join A squares to ends of two remaining E/F units. Join rows to assemble star. Block should measure approximately 12½" square.

4. Make seven blocks with red star points and blue logs. In same manner, make eight blocks with blue star points and red logs (see **Block 3 Diagram**).

Diagram F

Quilt Assembly

Throughout assembly, keep red and blue fabrics positioned as shown in **Row Assembly Diagram**.

1. For Row 1, join three of Block 1 and two of Block 2 as shown. Make two of Row 1.

2. For Row 2, join two of Block 3 and one Block 4 as shown; then add a Block 2 to row ends. Make three of Row 2.

3. For Row 3, join two of Block 4 and one Block 3 as shown; then add a Block 1 to row ends. Make two of Row 3.

4. Referring to photo, lay out rows 1-2-3-2-3-2-1. Check placement of blocks and fabric colors. Join rows in order to assemble quilt.

Quilting and Finishing

1. Mark quilting design on quilt top as desired. Quilt shown is outline-quilted with an allover clamshell design on the background fabric.

2. Divide backing into two equal lengths. Cut one piece in half lengthwise. Join a narrow panel to each side of wide piece to assemble backing.

3. Layer backing, batting, and quilt top. Baste. Quilt as desired.

4. Make 8½ yards of bias or straight-grain binding. See page 156 for instructions on making and applying binding.

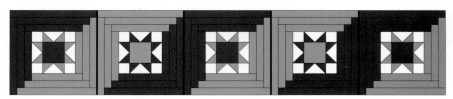

Row 1—Make 2.

Row 2—Make 3.

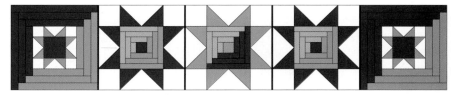

Row 3—Make 2.

Row Assembly Diagram

Size Variations

	Full/Queen	King
Finished Size	84" x 84"	108" x 108"
Number of		
Block 1	12	16
Block 2	12	16
Block 3	13	25
Block 4	12	24
Blocks Set	7 x 7	9 x 9
Yardage Required		
Red scraps	3⅜ yards	6¼ yards
Blue scraps	3⅜ yards	6¼ yards
Tan scraps	¾ yard	1⅜ yards
Background fabric	3⅜ yards	6 yards
Binding fabric	⅞ yard	1 yard
Backing fabric	6⅛ yards	10 yards

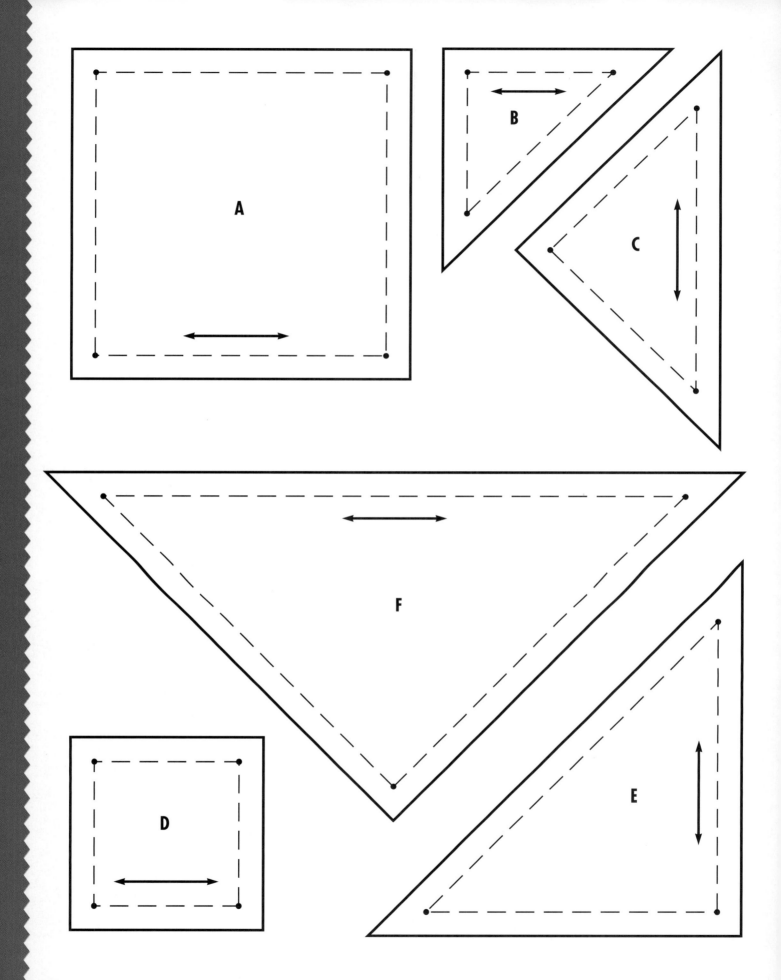

spools

Quiltmakers have a passion for sewing tools, so we honor our crafting heritage with this easy-to-sew traditional block. Old-fashioned wooden spools are now much prized by antique collectors. In pioneer days, a homemaker wrapped her homespun thread and yarn on these spools to keep them clean and tangle-free until the next weaving day.

Finished Size

Quilt: 66" x 78"
Blocks: 143 blocks, 6" x 6"
This quilt fits a twin-size bed. See Size Variations (page 75) for other size requirements.

Materials

½ yard *each* of seven light prints
72 (6" x 17") medium/dark fabrics or equivalent scraps
¾ yard binding fabric
4 yards backing fabric
72" x 90" precut batting

Quilt by Carole Collins of Norfolk, Nebraska

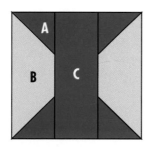

Spools Block—Make 143.

Making Blocks

Instructions are for rotary cutting and quick piecing. For traditional techniques, use patterns on page 75.

1. From one ½ yard of light fabric, cut seven 2½"-wide cross-grain strips. From these, cut 42 (2½" x 6½") B rectangles. Repeat with remaining light fabrics to get 286 Bs, two for each block.
2. From one dark fabric, cut two 2½" x 17" strips. (*Note:* For traditional cutting, use templates instead of cutting strips.) From one strip, cut four 2½" A squares and one 2½" x 6½" C rectangle for your first block. Select two Bs to go with these pieces.
3. Referring to page 146, use the diagonal-corner technique to sew two A squares to each B rectangle **(Diagram A)**. Or sew A triangles to B traditionally as shown. Make two A/B units for each block. Press seam allowances toward triangles.
4. Join A/B units to sides of C as shown **(Block Assembly Diagram)**. Press seam allowances toward C.
5. Make 143 Spools blocks in this manner.

Quilt Assembly

1. Lay out 11 blocks in a horizontal row. Turn alternating blocks on their sides as shown **(Row Assembly Diagram)**. Row 1 starts and ends with upright blocks. Row 2 starts and ends with turned blocks. Lay out 13 rows, alternating rows 1 and 2.
2. When blocks are laid out in rows, rearrange them to achieve a pleasing balance of color and value. When satisfied with placement, join blocks in each row.
3. Referring to photo, join rows.

Quilting and Finishing

1. Mark quilting design on quilt top as desired. Quilt shown has diagonal lines quilted on each block, spaced ¾" apart.
2. Divide backing into two equal lengths. Cut one piece in half lengthwise. Sew narrow panels to sides of wide piece to assemble backing.
3. Layer backing, batting, and quilt top. Backing seams will run parallel to top and bottom edges of quilt. Baste. Quilt as desired.
4. Make 9 yards of bias or straight-grain binding. See page 156 for instructions on making and applying binding.

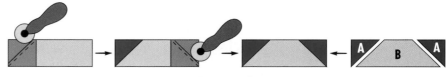

Diagram A

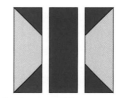

Block Assembly Diagram

Row 1—Make 7.

Row 2—Make 6.

Row Assembly Diagram

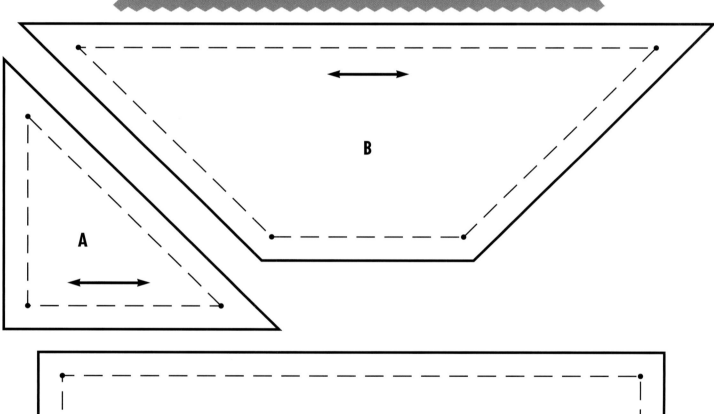

Size Variations			
	Full	**Queen**	**King**
Finished Size	78" x 90"	90" x 102"	102" x 102"
Number of Blocks	195	255	289
Blocks Set	13 x 15	15 x 17	17 x 17
Yardage Required			
Light ½ yards	10	12	14
Dark scraps	98	128	145
Binding fabric	⅞ yard	1 yard	1 yard
Backing fabric	2¾ yards	2¾ yards	3 yards
	(90" wide)	(108" wide)	(108" wide)

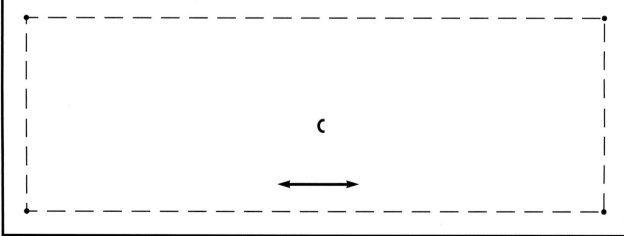

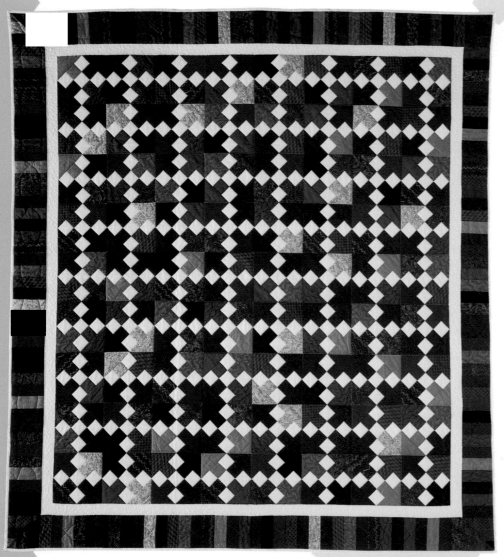

Quilt by Jane Ross of Fairhope, Alabama

Nine squares in a tic-tac-toe formation make one of patch-work's basic building blocks—the versatile nine-patch. In this variation, the nine-patch is turned on point in each block so the muslin squares connect in continuous chains across the quilt.

This sparkling quilt combines bright tone-on-tone prints with muslin, but it's fun to dream up other color schemes. Think about mixed pastels with a purple chain. Or scraps of blue with a yellow chain. Or pink and green. The possibilities are as varied as your scraps.

Finished Size

Quilt: 84" x 92"
Blocks: 72 blocks, 8½" x 8½"
This quilt fits a queen-size bed. See Size Variations (page 78) for other size requirements.

Materials

⅜ yard *each* of 18 print fabrics
2¼ yards muslin
¾ yard binding fabric
2½ yards 108"-wide backing fabric
90" x 108" precut batting

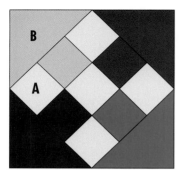

Crossroads to Jericho Block—Make 72.

Making Blocks

Instructions are for rotary cutting. For traditional cutting, use patterns on page 78.

1. From each print fabric, cut three 2½" crosswise strips, one for strip piecing the nine-patch and two for outer border pieces. From remainder of each fabric, cut eight 5⅛" squares. Cut each square in half diagonally to get 16 B triangles.

2. From muslin, cut 31 (2½"-wide) cross-grain strips. Set aside eight strips for inner border.

3. For Strip Set 1, join one strip of print fabric and two muslin strips as shown (**Strip Set 1 Diagram**). Press seam allowances toward print strip. Make nine of Strip Set 1.

4. For Strip Set 2, join two strips of print fabric and one muslin strip as shown (**Strip Set 2 Diagram**). Press seam allowances toward print strips. Make five of Strip Set 2.

5. From each strip set, rotary-cut 16 (2½"-wide) segments as shown to get a total of 144 Strip Set 1 segments and 72 Strip Set 2 segments (and eight extra).

6. For each block, select two Strip Set 1 segments and one Strip Set 2 segment. Join segments to form a nine-patch (**Nine-Patch Diagram**). Make 72 nine-patches.

7. Select a nine-patch for the first block. Find a B triangle that matches each print fabric. Sew a triangle to two opposite sides of nine-patch, matching fabrics as shown (**Block Assembly Diagram**). Press seam allowances toward triangles. Add triangles to remaining sides to complete block.

8. Make 72 blocks.

Quilt Assembly

1. Lay out blocks in nine rows of eight blocks each. Arrange blocks to get a pleasing balance of color and value. When satisfied with placement, join blocks in each row (**Row Assembly Diagram**).

2. Referring to photo, join rows.

Borders

1. Join two muslin strips end-to-end for each inner border.

2. Referring to page 150, measure quilt from top to bottom and trim two borders to match length. Sew borders to quilt sides.

3. Measure quilt from side to side and trim remaining borders to match quilt width. Sew borders to top and bottom edges of quilt.

4. For outer border, cut 176 (2½" x 6½") Cs from remaining strips of print fabric. Referring to photo, join 46 Cs in a row for each side border and 42 Cs each for top and bottom borders. Referring to page 151, sew borders to quilt and miter corners.

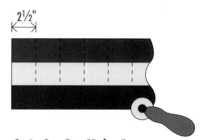

Strip Set 1—Make 9.   **Strip Set 2—Make 5.**

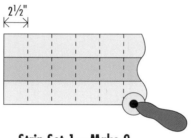

Nine-Patch Diagram

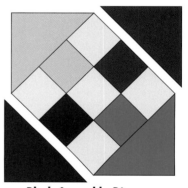

Block Assembly Diagram

Row Assembly Diagram

Quilting and Finishing

1. Mark quilting design on quilt top as desired. The quilt shown is machine-quilted with outline quilting in the blocks, stipple quilting in inner border, and a wide cable in outer border.
2. Layer backing, batting, and quilt top. Baste. Quilt as desired.
3. Make 10 yards of bias or straight-grain binding. See page 156 for instructions on making and applying binding.

Size Variations

	Twin	Full	King
Finished Size	66" x 92"	76" x 92"	100" x 100"
Number of Blocks	54	63	100
Blocks Set	6 x 9	7 x 9	10 x 10
Number of			
Strip Set 1	7	8	12½
Strip Set 2	3½	4	6½
C pieces	158	168	200

Yardage Required

	Twin	Full	King
⅜-yard print fabrics	14	16	26
Muslin	2 yards	2 yards	2⅞ yards
Binding fabric	¾ yard	¾ yard	⅞ yard
108"-wide backing fabric	2 yards	2⅜ yards	3 yards

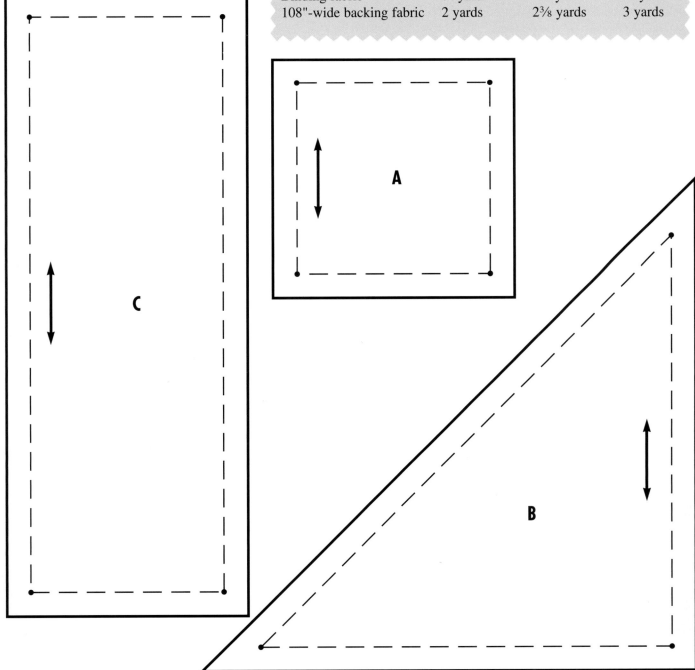

signs & symbols

Fusible appliqué helps you make this quilt in what will seem like a flash! This technique is fast and fun, and your quilt is sturdy enough for the hazards of real life. Or appliqué traditionally, if you like. See page 82 for fusible appliqué instructions and page 83 for color options.

Finished Size

Quilt: 38" x 38"
Blocks: 64 blocks, 3¾" x 3¾"
This quilt is wall hanging or crib-size. See Size Variations (page 83) for bed-size requirements.

Materials

100 (4¼") squares
Scraps for appliqué
½ yard binding fabric
1¼ yards backing fabric
42" x 42" batting
Paper-backed fusible web
   (optional)

Quilt by Christine L. Adams of Rockville, Maryland

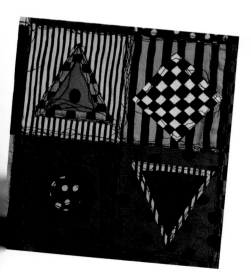

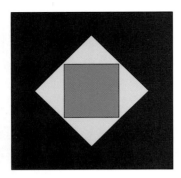  

Signs & Symbols Blocks—Make 64.

Choosing Fabrics

For an effective quilt, choose a fabric theme. Christine chose geometrics—stripes, checks, and dots in a rainbow of colors. You might prefer plaids with tone-on-tone prints or stripes alternating with floral prints. Experiment!

You might base your fabric theme on color. Pastels or primary colors are good choices for a child's quilt, while red fabrics and green fabrics evoke thoughts of Christmas. See page 83 for more color suggestions.

In addition to Christine's geometric shapes, we've added optional patterns for stars and hearts to give you more flexibility with your quilt theme.

Manufacturers produce lines of companion fabrics that are ideal for a quilt like this—you can buy ⅛ yard of each fabric in the line and you're instantly coordinated. But it's more challenging to mix and match your own fabrics, looking for the right balance of color, value, and scale.

Quilt Top Assembly

Instructions are for rotary cutting and fusible appliqué. Before cutting, read instructions below and on opposite page to decide whether you prefer fusible or traditional appliqué. Appliqué patterns are on page 84.

1. Following instructions on page 82, trace desired shapes onto paper side of fusible web. Cut out web pieces, leaving a small amount of paper around each outline.
2. Fuse web to wrong side of each scrap fabric. Cut out appliqués on drawn line.

3. Set aside 36 (4¼") squares for borders. Fuse appliqués onto 64 squares as desired, mixing different shapes and fabrics. (*Quiltmaker's Note:* Christine says, "I just stick fabric on the foundation until the colors and shapes please me. The pieces are small, so you can use bits of children's clothing or something of your grandmother's to make the quilt really meaningful.")
4. Add finishing to appliqués if desired (see PinPoints on page 82 for finishing suggestions). Christine added topstitching after she

joined her blocks (see Step 1, Quilting and Finishing).
5. Lay out appliqué blocks in eight rows with eight blocks in each row (**Quilt Assembly Diagram**). Arrange blocks to get a pleasing balance of color, value, and shape.
6. When satisfied with placement, join blocks in each row.
7. Join rows as shown.
8. Join eight squares in a row for top border. Sew border to top edge of quilt. Repeat for bottom border.
9. Join 10 squares in a vertical row for each side border. Sew borders to quilt sides.

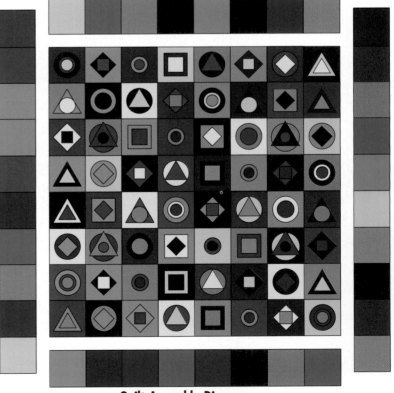

Quilt Assembly Diagram

Quilting and Finishing

1. To topstitch assembled quilt top, Christine used black thread throughout. She outlined each shape, sewing squiggly stitching lines back and forth over seams and around each appliqué. The more wobbly the stitching, the more creative you are! If traditional quilting is desired, mark quilting design on quilt top.

2. Layer backing, batting, and quilt top. Baste. Quilt as desired. On wall hanging shown, machine quilting through all layers is limited to outline of border blocks. For a bed-size quilt, more quilting is necessary to hold layers together appropriately.

3. Make 4½ yards of 3½"-wide straight-grain binding. See page 156 for instructions on making and applying binding.

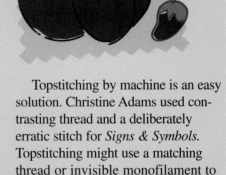

Fusible Appliqué

Paper-backed fusible web is a heat-activated adhesive with a temporary paper lining. Heated with a hot iron, fusible web secures shapes to a background fabric, eliminating the need for basting as in traditional appliqué.

Use lightweight web to appliqué quilts or wall hangings. For washable items, heavy-duty web might be better. When you use fusible web, read the label for tips on use and washing. Available brands of paper-backed web are Pellon® WonderUnder, Aleene's Fusible Web™, and HeatnBond®.

Before fusing, always prewash fabrics to remove sizing, which prevents fusible web from bonding with fabric.

Patterns for Fusible Appliqué

Paper-backed web is translucent, so you can lay it directly on a pattern for tracing. This lets you use any printed material as a pattern. Pattern sources include wrapping paper, coloring books, and greeting cards. The kitchen is full of circles and cookie cutters to trace. Even hands and feet are potential patterns. If a tracing isn't the size you want, use a photocopy machine to enlarge or reduce it.

If a shape is not symmetrical (that is, if it must point one way or the other), remember that the finished appliqué is a mirror image of your drawing. If you want the piece to face its original direction, copy the drawing on tracing paper; then darken the image on *both* sides of the tracing paper so you can trace either direction onto the paper-backed web.

Fusing

With a pencil, trace motif onto paper (smooth) side of web **(Photo A)**. Use paper scissors to cut around motif, leaving a small amount of paper around the tracing.

Place adhesive (rough) side of web on *wrong* side of appliqué fabric. Following package instructions, use a dry iron to fuse web to fabric **(Photo B)**. Do not overheat. Some manufacturers recommend a pressing cloth between iron and appliqué to avoid getting stray fibers of sticky stuff on the iron.

Let fabric cool. Cut out motif on drawn line. If desired, use pinking shears for a jagged edge.

Peel off paper backing **(Photo C)**. If backing is difficult to remove, use a needle or pin to loosen one corner.

Position appliqué on background fabric. Be sure of placement before you fuse, following manufacturer's instructions. If you have several layers of appliqué, lightly press each piece in place. When all layers are correctly positioned, fuse them together with more heat **(Photo D)**.

Finishing Edges

Fusible web holds appliqués in place through many washings, but inevitably fraying will occur, especially on a garment or quilt that is used daily. For best results, finish the appliqué edges.

Topstitching by machine is an easy solution. Christine Adams used contrasting thread and a deliberately erratic stitch for *Signs & Symbols*. Topstitching might use a matching thread or invisible monofilament to closely outline the shape with a straight or zigzag machine stitch.

A machine satin stitch puts a ridge of tight stitches around each piece, giving the shape strong definition. But be warned—machine appliqué requires skill in sewing corners, points, and curves.

Buttonhole stitch, worked by hand or machine, adds decoration to the work. See page 105 for tips on Buttonhole-Stitch Appliqué.

Another finish, used mostly on garments, is washable fabric paint. These are available at craft stores in squeeze tubes that put a thin line of paint around an appliqué.

A

B

C

D

Color Consciousness

Color choices determine the personality of a quilt as much as fabric patterns.
Here are some suggestions for *Signs & Symbols* of a different tone.

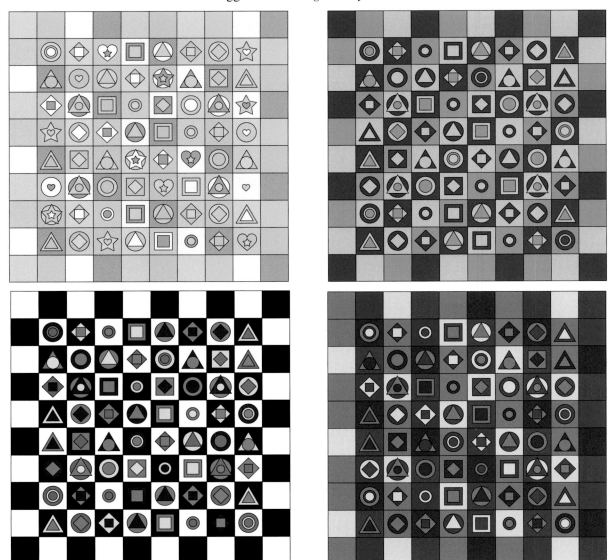

Size Variations*

	Twin	Full	Queen	King
Finished Size*	60" x 96"	78" x 96"	84" x 102"	102" x 102"
Appliquéd Blocks*	112	154	180	225
Blocks Set	8 x 14	11 x 14	12 x 15	15 x 15
Yardage Required				
6½" squares*	160	206	242	289
Binding fabric	1 yard	1 yard	1⅛ yards	1⅛ yards
108"-wide backing fabric	2 yards	2⅜ yards	2½ yards	3 yards

*Note: To maintain appropriate scale, a larger block is desirable for bed-size quilts.
 For these sizes, start with a 6½" base square (finished size 6"). On a photocopy
machine, enlarge appliqué patterns 160%.

Geometric Patterns

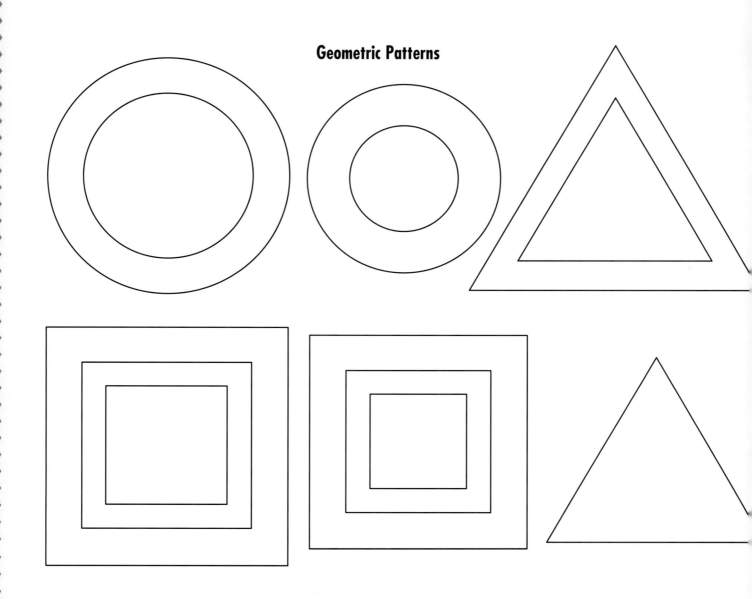

Optional Patterns

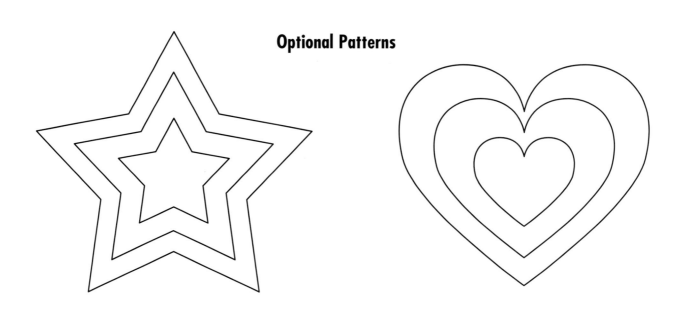

stars in motion

Like most things, quiltmaking is more fun when you share it with a friend. Three friends collaborated on this quilt, which alternates Shoo Fly blocks and star-like Water Wheel blocks. Subtle tone-on-tone neutral fabrics provide a nicely textured background for bright prints.

Finished Size

Quilt: 69" x 87"
Blocks: 63 blocks, 9" x 9"
This quilt fits a twin-size bed. See Size Variations (page 87) for other size requirements.

Materials

63 (4" x 12") pieces of print fabrics
10 (½-yard) pieces of beige/tan fabrics
¾ yard binding fabric
5⅜ yards backing fabric
72" x 90" precut batting

Quilt by Judie Herzog, Carolyn Koopman, and Shirley Peterman of Fairfield, Iowa; quilted by Vi Winter

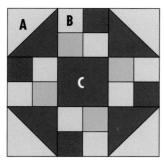

Shoo Fly Block—Make 32.

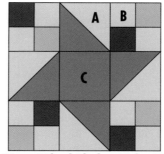

Water Wheel Block—Make 31.

Making Blocks

Instructions are for rotary cutting. For traditional cutting, use patterns A, B, and C on page 88.

1. From each print fabric, cut two 3⅞" squares for triangle-squares and one 3½" C square.

2. From assorted beige fabrics, cut 12 (3⅞"-wide) cross-grain strips. From these, cut 126 (3⅞") squares. On wrong side of each square, draw a diagonal line from corner to corner.

3. Match each beige square with a same-size square of print fabric, right sides facing. Sew through both layers, ¼" from both sides of drawn line (Diagram A). Press seam; then rotary-cut on drawn line to get two triangle-squares as shown. Press seam allowances toward print fabric. Make four triangle-squares for each block, a total of 252. *Note:* The print fabrics should match in each block, but you can vary background fabrics of triangle-squares as desired.

4. From remaining beige fabrics, cut 64 (2"-wide) cross-grain strips.

5. With right sides facing, join two beige strips along one long edge. Press seam allowances toward dark fabric. Rotary-cut 22 (2"-wide) segments from each strip set (Diagram B). Make 32 strip sets and cut a total of 704 (2"-wide) segments.

6. Select any two segments for your first four-patch. Join segments as

shown (Diagram C). Make 353 four-patch units. Press. Set aside 100 units for border.

7. For one Shoo Fly block, select four four-patches, four triangle-squares, and one C square, matching print fabric. Join units in three rows as shown (Shoo Fly Block Assembly Diagram). Press seam allowances away from four-patches. Join rows to complete block. Make 32 Shoo Fly blocks.

8. For a Water Wheel block, select four triangle-squares, four four-patches, and a C square, matching

print fabric. Join units in three rows as shown (Water Wheel Block Assembly Diagram). Press seam allowances away from four-patches. Join rows to complete block. Make 31 Water Wheel blocks.

Quilt Assembly

1. Join three four-patches in a row to make one border unit (Diagram D). Make 32 border units, leaving four four-patches left over.

2. Lay out blocks in nine horizontal rows of seven blocks each, alternating Shoo Fly and Water Wheel blocks as shown (Row Assembly Diagram). Lay out five of Row 1, starting with a Shoo Fly block, and four of Row 2, starting with a Water Wheel block. Add a border unit to both ends of each row.

3. Arrange blocks to get a pleasing balance of color and value. When satisfied with placement, join blocks in each row.

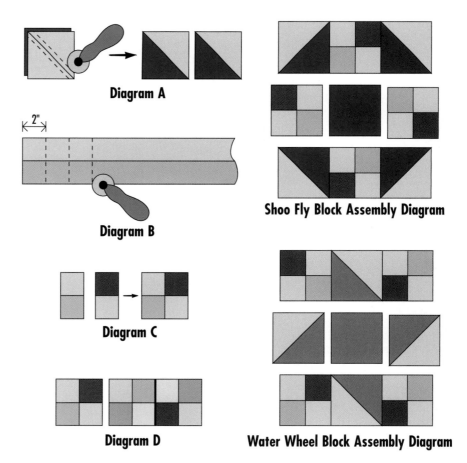

Diagram A

Diagram B

Diagram C

Diagram D

Shoo Fly Block Assembly Diagram

Water Wheel Block Assembly Diagram

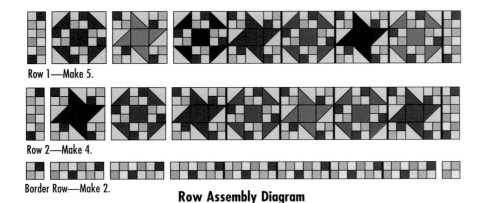

Row 1—Make 5.

Row 2—Make 4.

Border Row—Make 2.

Row Assembly Diagram

4. Referring to photo, join rows.
5. For Border Row, join remaining border units in two rows of seven units each as shown. Add a four-patch to ends of each row. Sew a Border Row to top and bottom edges of quilt top.

Quilting and Finishing

1. Mark a quilting design on quilt top as desired. Quilt shown has outline quilting in the blocks and diagonal lines of quilting that cross in an X through the center of each four-patch.
2. Divide backing into two equal lengths. Cut one piece in half lengthwise. Join narrow panels to sides of wide piece to assemble backing.
3. Layer backing, batting, and quilt top. Baste. Quilt as desired.
4. Make 9 yards of bias or straight-grain binding. See page 156 for instructions on making and applying binding.

Size Variations

	Full	Queen	King
Finished Size	78" x 96"	87" x 96"	96" x 96"
Number of Blocks	80	90	100
Blocks Set	8 x 10	9 x 10	10 x 10
Number of			
Strip Sets	40	44	48
Four-Patch Units	432	478	520
Border Units	36	38	40
Yardage Required			
4" x 12" print scraps	80	90	100
½-yard beige fabrics	13	14	15
Binding fabric	⅞ yard	⅞ yard	1 yard
108"-wide backing fabric	2 yards	2⅜ yards	3 yards

pinpoints

Signature Patch

When you sign and date a quilt, you send a little of yourself into the future. Most antique quilts are anonymous, like empty pages where there should be history about people and family. Future generations will appreciate having a record of who made each quilt and why.

There are several ways to permanently mark a quilt, on the front or back. The most popular is a signature patch, sometimes called a memory patch, that is sewn onto the backing.

This label might include your name, town, the date on which the quilt was completed, who it was made for, and any special occasion connected with it. You can also add washing instructions for the benefit of future owners.

A practical label is a piece of muslin, hemmed on all sides. To stabilize the fabric for writing, press freezer paper to the back, coated side against the muslin. Use a fine-tip permanent pen to write your message; then peel off the paper and handstitch the label to the quilt back.

You can use embroidery and cross-stitch to make a lovely signature patch. Incorporating a name and date in the quilting is another time-honored method.

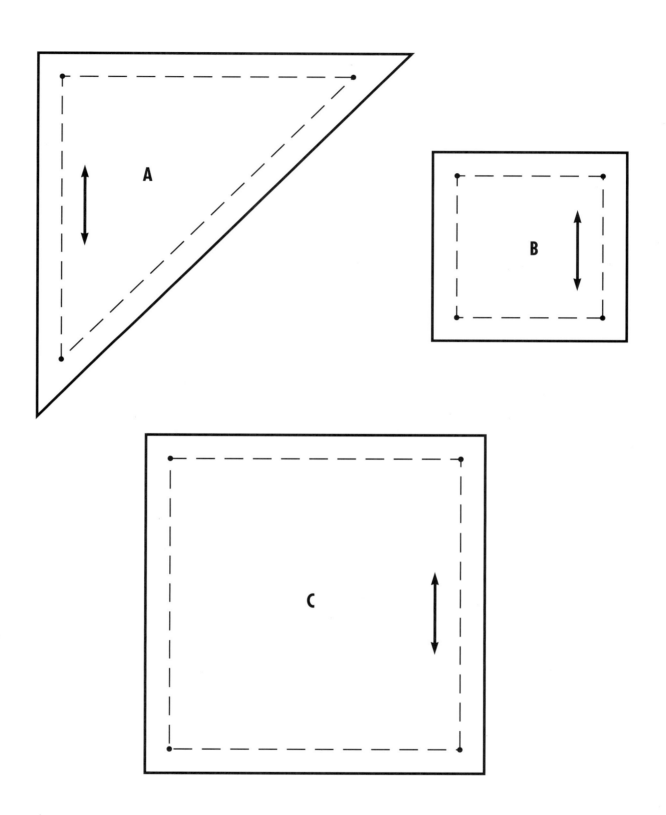

spring blossoms

Pastels aplenty make this quilt springtime fresh. The block, a variation of the classic Ohio Star, is the result of a Block Exchange, a swap in which each participant makes blocks for her friends. Winnie Fleming's request for pastel fabrics produced these lovely blocks. Since everyone's fabric choices are different, no two blocks are the same.

Finished Size

Quilt: 67" x 85"
Blocks: 48 blocks, 9" x 9"
This quilt fits a twin-size bed. See Size Variations (page 92) for other size requirements.

Materials

48 (4" x 8") print scraps
48 (9" x 14") print scraps
½ yard *each* of 8 white-on-white print fabrics
1¼ yards inner border fabric (includes binding)
2½ yards outer border fabric
5⅛ yards backing fabric
72" x 90" precut batting

Quilt by Winnie S. Fleming of Houston, Texas; machine-quilted by Lenel Walsh

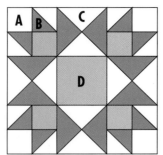

Spring Blossoms Block—Make 48.

Making Blocks

Instructions are for rotary cutting and quick piecing. Before cutting, read block instructions and decide whether you prefer quick piecing or traditional piecing. For traditional cutting, use patterns on page 92.

1. Cut 48 (9" x 14") white pieces, three from each fabric.
2. For one block, select a piece of white fabric and one each of 9" x 14" and 4" x 8" print scraps. From white fabric, cut a 7" square for B triangle-squares, two 4¼" squares for C triangle-squares, and four 2" A squares. From 9" x 14" print fabric, cut a 7" square and two 4¼" squares.
3. On wrong side of 7" white square, draw a two-square by two-square grid of 2⅜" squares (**Diagram A**). Mark diagonal lines through centers of squares as shown.
4. Match marked square with 7" print square, right sides facing. Stitch on both sides of diagonal lines, pivoting at grid corners as shown. Press. Cut on all drawn lines to get eight B triangle-squares. Press seam allowances toward print fabric.
5. Referring to PinPoints on page 91, use 4¼" squares to make four C Hourglass triangle-squares.
6. From 4" x 8" scrap, cut four 2" A squares and one 3½" D square.
7. For each corner unit, select two B triangle-squares and one A square

each of white and print fabrics. Sew triangle-squares to A squares as shown (**Diagram B**). Join to make a four-patch corner unit. Make four corner units for the block.

8. Arrange corner units, Hourglass units, and D square in three rows as shown (**Block Assembly Diagram**). Join units in each row; then join rows to complete block.
9. Make 48 Spring Blossoms blocks. In 24 blocks, press seam allowances toward the corner units; in the remaining 24 blocks, press seam allowances away from the corner units. This results in offset seam allowances when you join blocks in rows.

Quilt Assembly

1. Lay out blocks in eight horizontal rows with six blocks in each row (**Row Assembly Diagram**). Arrange blocks to achieve a pleasing balance of color and value.
2. When satisfied with placement, join blocks in each row.
3. Referring to photo, join rows.

Borders

1. From inner border fabric, cut eight 2"-wide cross-grain strips. Join two strips end-to-end to make each border strip.
2. From outer border fabric, cut four 5½"-wide lengthwise strips.
3. Referring to pages 150 and 151, measure each quilt edge and mark borders. Sew borders to quilt edges and miter corners.

Quilting and Finishing

1. Mark quilting design on quilt top as desired. Quilt shown is machine-quilted with a meandering pattern of stipple quilting all over the quilt surface.
2. Divide backing into two equal lengths. Cut one in half lengthwise. Join narrow panels to sides of wide piece to make backing.
3. Layer backing, batting, and quilt top. Baste. Quilt as desired.
4. Use remaining border fabric to make 9 yards of bias or straight-grain binding. See page 156 for instructions on making and applying binding.

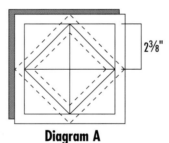

Diagram A

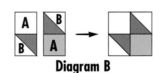

Diagram B

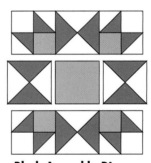

Block Assembly Diagram

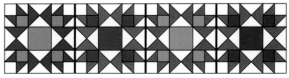

Row Assembly Diagram

Quick-Pieced Hourglass Units

A **patchwork square** comprised of four right-triangles is sometimes called an Hourglass block (or unit of a block). Traditionally, you would cut four triangles and sew them together to make a square. But if you need several units with the same two-fabric combination, it's easier, faster, and more accurate to quick-piece the blocks as described here.

These instructions are tailored to *Spring Blossoms,* but the technique can be applied to any patchwork that calls for Hourglass units or blocks.

Before you begin, there are two important points to remember when you use this quick-piecing technique:

* Always start with fabric squares that are 1¼" larger than the desired **finished** size of the unit.

* You get **two** Hourglass units from each pair of fabric squares.

1. For *Spring Blossoms,* use 4¼" squares of white and print fabrics to make Hourglass units.
2. On the wrong side of each white square, draw a diagonal line from corner to corner. With right sides facing, match the marked square with a square of scrap fabric.
3. Stitch a ¼" seam on *both* sides of the diagonal line (Diagram A). Press stitching.
4. Cut units apart on the drawn line between the stitching (Diagram B). Press units open, pressing the seam allowance toward the scrap fabric. You will have two triangle-squares (Diagram C).

5. On the wrong side of one triangle-square, draw a line from the corner of the white triangle to the corner of the scrap triangle. Then match both triangle-squares *with contrasting fabrics facing* and the marked unit on top.
6. Stitch a ¼" seam on *both* sides of the marked line (Diagram D).
7. Cut the units apart between the stitching lines as before (Diagram E). Press both squares open to get two Hourglass units (Diagram F). In this example, the sewn units now measure 3½" square (including seam allowances). When sewn into the *Spring Blossoms* block, the finished unit will be 3".

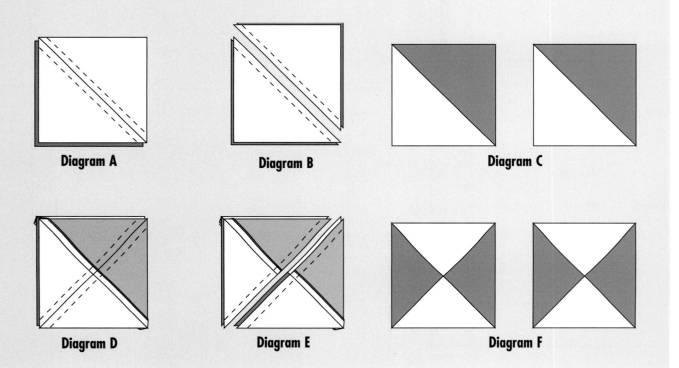

Diagram A **Diagram B** **Diagram C**

Diagram D **Diagram E** **Diagram F**

Size Variations

	Full	Queen	King
Finished Size	76" x 94"	85" x 103"	103" x 103"
Number of Blocks	63	80	100
Blocks Set	7 x 9	8 x 10	10 x 10
Yardage Required			
4" x 8" prints	63	80	100
9" x 14" prints	63	80	100
½ yards of white	11	14	17
Inner border fabric	1¼ yards	1⅜ yards	1½ yards
Outer border fabric	2¾ yards	3 yards	3 yards
Backing fabric	5⅝ yards	6 yards	9¼ yards

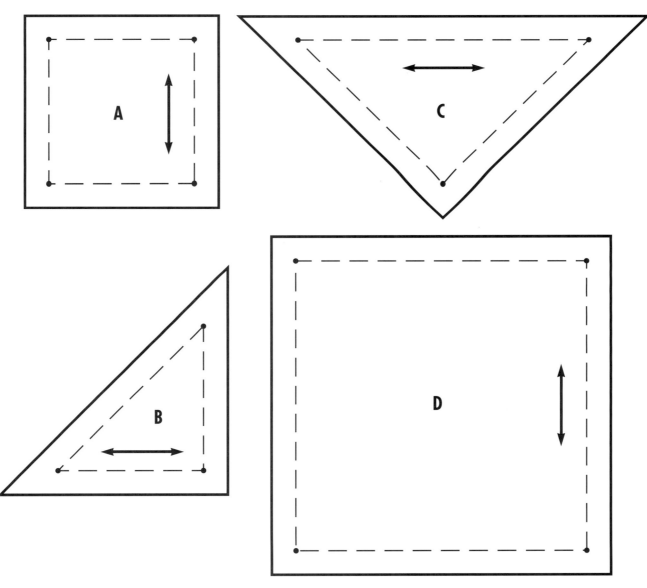

Sampler Suggestions

Making different blocks is one of the joys of quiltmaking. Each block is a new challenge. If you like to try new and interesting things, you'll enjoy making sampler quilts.

A sampler quilt combines different blocks with wonderful results. Use color as a unifying factor, especially when you use scraps.

The medallion-set sampler below left uses the Shoo Fly block from *Stars in Motion*, as well as blocks from *Spools* and *Baskets of Liberty*. The sampler below right shows blocks from (starting in the center) *Spider Web*, *Devil on the Run, Spools, Wildflowers*, and *Stars In, Stars Out*.

The sampler at right is a different set that uses blocks from eight quilts (starting at top left corner): *Crossed Canoes; Baskets of Liberty; Stars In, Stars Out; Stars in Motion; Corn & Beans; Prairie Queen; Spools;* and *Spring Blossoms.*

These samples show how you might use plain strips, checkerboard piecing, triangle-squares, and other units to fill in between blocks of different sizes.

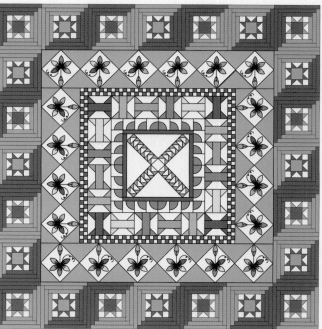

prairie queen

Quilt by Gerry Sweem of Reseda, California

Folksy plaids and peppy stripes make a delightful combination in this cozy quilt. Don't worry about matching plaids and stripes at the seams. Let the lines fall where they may; the mismatched quality adds an element of charm. This variation of the Prairie Queen block is also known as Cross & Chains, Richmond, and Aunt Vina's Favorite.

Finished Size

Quilt: 96½" x 96½"
Blocks: 60 blocks, 9" x 9"
This quilt fits a king-size bed. See Size Variations (page 98) for other size requirements.

Materials

30 fat quarters (18" x 22" pieces)
   light/medium fabrics
30 fat quarters (18" x 22" pieces)
   medium/dark fabrics
6 (16¾") squares light/medium
   fabrics or equivalent scraps
10 (⅛-yard) pieces red fabrics
1 yard binding fabric
3 yards 108"-wide backing fabric
120" x 120" precut batting

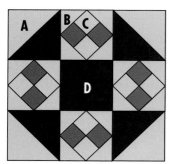

Prairie Queen Block — Make 60.

Making Blocks

Instructions are for rotary cutting and quick piecing. Before cutting, read block instructions and decide whether you prefer quick piecing or traditional piecing. For traditional cutting, use patterns on page 98.

1. From each dark fabric, cut two 6" x 10" pieces and two 3½" D squares. Set aside remainder for sashing.

2. From each light fabric, cut two 6" x 10" pieces, two 1⅝" x 13½" strips, and 16 (2½") squares. Cut squares in half diagonally to get 32 B triangles. Set aside remaining fabric for sashing squares.

3. From red fabrics, cut 60 (1⅝" x 13½") strips.

4. For one block, select a 6" x 10" piece, 16 B triangles, and one 1⅝" strip of the same light fabric. Then choose a 6" x 10" piece and a D square of one dark fabric, and one 1⅝" strip of red fabric. Each fabric will appear in at least two blocks, but avoid repeating the same combination.

5. On wrong side of 6" x 10" light fabric, mark a two-square grid of 3⅞" squares as shown (**Diagram A**). Mark diagonal lines through squares as shown. Match marked fabric with dark fabric piece, right sides facing. Stitch on both sides of diagonal lines as shown. Press stitching; then cut on drawn lines to get four A

triangle-squares. Press seam allowances toward dark fabric.

6. Sewing a generous ¼" seam, join 1⅝"-wide strips as shown (**Diagram B**). Press seam allowance toward red fabric. From this, cut eight 1⅝"-wide segments as shown. Again sewing a generous ¼" seam, join two segments to make a four-patch (**Diagram C**). Make four four-patches.

7. Sew B triangles to two opposite sides of each four-patch as shown (**Diagram D**). Press seam allowances toward triangles. Sew B triangles to remaining sides of four-patch.

8. You now have nine 3½"-square units for the block—four A triangle-squares, four B/C four-patches, and one dark D square. Arrange units in rows as shown (**Block Assembly Diagram**), checking to be sure four-patch units are turned

to position red squares as shown. Join units in each row. Press seam allowances toward dark fabrics. Then join rows to complete block.

9. Make 60 Prairie Queen blocks.

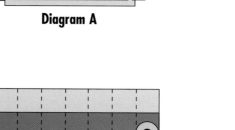

Diagram A

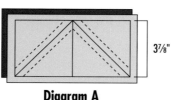

Diagram B

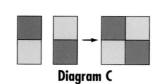

Diagram C

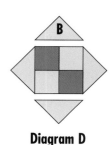

Diagram D

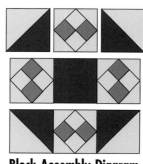

Block Assembly Diagram

Quilt Assembly

1. Cut each 16¾" square in quarters diagonally to get 24 setting triangles. From remaining dark fabrics, cut four 2½" x 14" and 140 (2½" x 9½") sashing strips. From light fabrics, cut 81 (2½") E sashing squares.

2. For Row 1, join 10 blocks with sashing strips between blocks (**Quilt Assembly Diagram**). For matching sashing row, join 10 sashing strips and 11 squares end-to-end as shown. Press seam allowances toward sashing in both rows. Join sashing row to block row; then sew setting triangles to both ends of row as shown.

3. For Row 2, join eight blocks with sashing strips between blocks as shown. Join eight sashing strips and nine sashing squares to make matching sashing row. Join block row and sashing row; then add setting triangles to row ends.

4. Continue joining blocks and sashing in diagonal rows, making rows 1–5 as shown.

5. For Row 6, sew a setting triangle to each side of one 14" sashing strip, matching bottom edges as shown. Sashing strip will be longer than triangles. Press seam allowances toward sashing. Trim excess sashing at corner, using edge of triangles as cutting guideline (Diagram E).

6. **Quilt Assembly Diagram** shows half of quilt. Repeat steps 2–5 above to make a second set of rows.

7. Referring to assembly diagram and photo on page 97, join rows 1–6. Repeat to assemble a second set of rows 1–6.

8. For center sashing row, join 11 sashing squares and 10 sashing strips end-to-end as shown. Add 14" sashing strips at each end of row. Press seam allowances toward sashing.

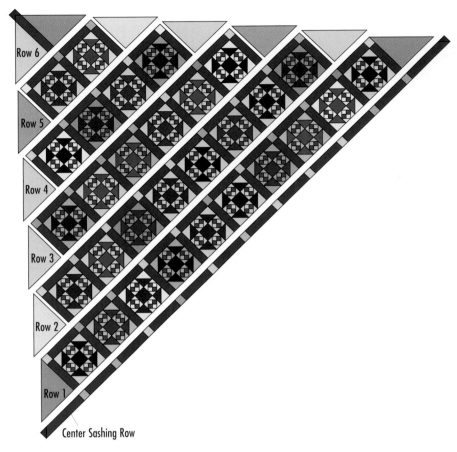

Quilt Assembly Diagram

9. Join quilt halves to sides of center sashing row, matching seams at sashing squares. When rows are joined, trim ends of center sashing row at quilt corners.

Quilting and Finishing

1. Mark quilting design on quilt top as desired. Quilt shown has straight lines of quilting, spaced 1⅜" apart, in one direction only (**Quilting Diagram**). Lines go through blocks and sashing strips, and extend into setting triangles.

2. Layer backing, batting, and quilt top. Baste. Quilt as desired.

3. Make 11 yards of bias or straight-grain binding. See page 156 for instructions on making and applying binding.

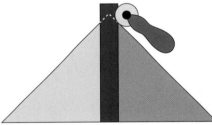

Diagram E

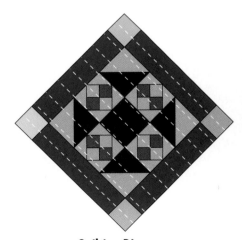

Quilting Diagram

Size Variations

	Twin	Full/Queen
Finished Size	65" x 96½"	81" x 96½"
Number of Blocks	38	49
Blocks Set	4 x 6	5 x 6
9½"-long sashing strips	92	116
Sashing Squares	55	68
Setting Triangles	20	22

Yardage Required

Light fat quarters	19	25
Dark fat quarters	19	25
16¾" squares	5	6
⅛-yard red pieces	13	17
Binding fabric	⅞ yard	⅞ yard
Backing fabric	6 yards	6 yards

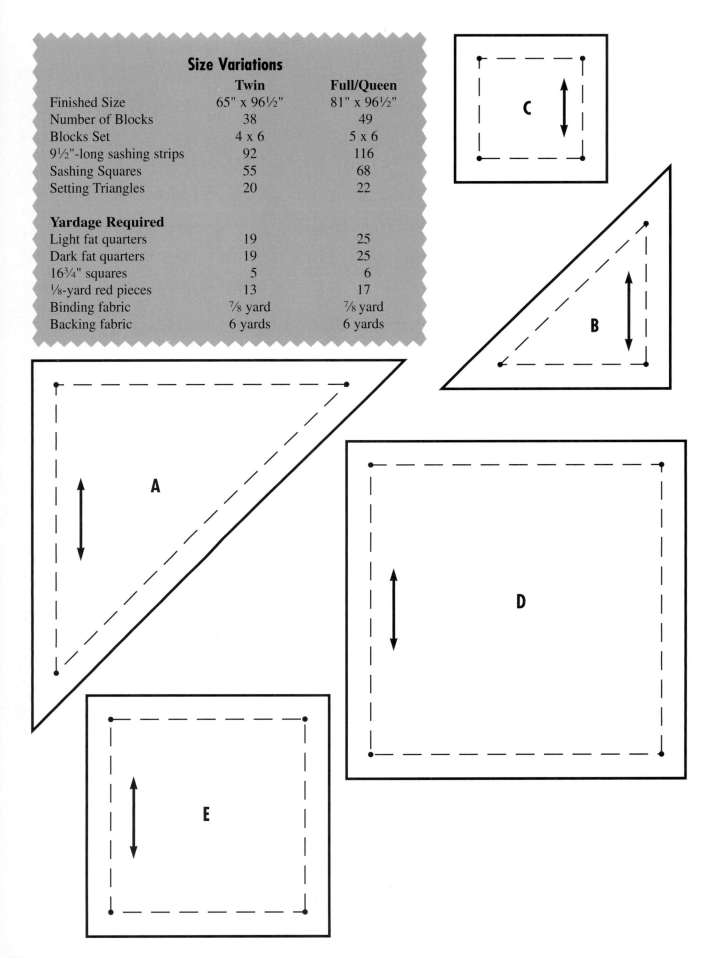

HUNter's star

ow do you turn one block into another? With quick-piecing techniques and clever placement, Robin Brower's Indian Arrowhead blocks are transformed into a variation of another block, the traditional Hunter's Star. Instead of cutting and piecing tricky diamonds, this method uses only squares and rectangles.

Finished Size

Quilt: 76" x 92"
Blocks: 80 blocks, 8" x 8"
This quilt fits a full-size bed. See Size Variations (page 101) for other size requirements.

Materials

¼ yard *each* of 27 print fabrics
5 yards muslin
⅞ yard binding fabric
5½ yards backing fabric
81" x 96" precut batting

Quilt by Robin Miller Brower of New Castle, Alabama; owned by Jimm Brower

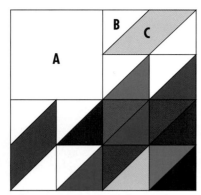

Indian Arrowhead Block—Make 80.

Making Blocks

Instructions are for rotary cutting and quick piecing. Before cutting, read block instructions and decide whether you prefer quick piecing or traditional piecing. For traditional cutting, use patterns on page 102.

1. From scrap fabrics, cut 60 (8" x 14") pieces for B triangle-squares and 160 (2½" x 4½") C pieces.

2. From muslin, cut four 6½" x 85" lengthwise strips for borders and set aside. Cut 20 (8" x 14") pieces for B triangle-squares, 80 (4½") A squares, and 160 (2½") B squares.

3. On wrong side of 8" x 14" muslin piece, draw a two-square by four-square grid of 2⅞" squares (**Diagram A**). Mark diagonal lines through squares as shown.

4. Match marked fabric piece with a scrap fabric, right sides facing. Starting at middle of one side, stitch on both sides of diagonal lines, pivoting at grid corners as shown. (Blue line in diagram shows one continuous stitching line; red shows second line.) Press. Cut on all drawn lines to get 16 triangle-squares from grid.

5. Following steps 3 and 4, stitch 20 muslin/scrap grids to get a total of 320 muslin/scrap triangle-squares. Follow the same steps to stitch 20 scrap/scrap grids to get a total of 320 scrap/scrap triangle-squares. Press seam allowances toward darker fabric.

6. Referring to page 146, use the diagonal-corner technique to sew two 2½" muslin B squares to a C (**Diagram B**). Or sew B triangles to C traditionally as shown. Make 160 B/C units. Press seam allowances toward Cs.

7. Join two muslin/scrap triangle-squares, sewing colored side of one to muslin side of second (**Diagram C**). Join pair to a B/C unit as shown. Make 160 units.

8. Join scrap/scrap triangle-squares in pairs (**Diagram D**); then join pairs to make a four-patch. Make 80 four-patch units as shown.

9. For one block, select an A square, two B/C units, and one scrap triangle-square unit (**Block Assembly Diagram**). Join units in two rows as shown; then join rows to complete block. Make 80 blocks. Lay out blocks in rows as you finish each one (**Row Assembly Diagram**). To make the stars come out, you'll want to select matching B/C units for the adjoining block(s).

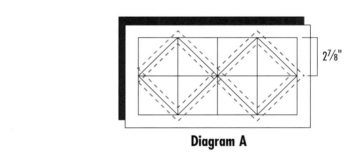

2⅞"

Diagram A

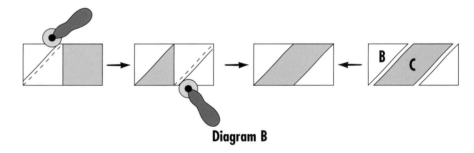

Diagram B

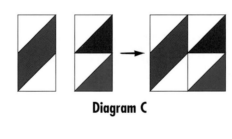

Diagram C

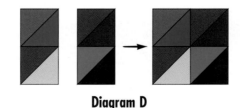

Diagram D

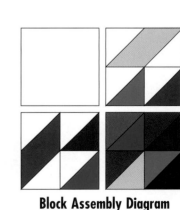

Block Assembly Diagram

Quilt Assembly

1. Lay out blocks in 10 horizontal rows with eight blocks in each row **(Row Assembly Diagram)**. Referring to diagram and photo, turn blocks to achieve star pattern.
2. When satisfied with placement, join blocks in each row.
3. Referring to photo, join rows.

Borders

1. Referring to page 150, measure quilt from top to bottom and trim two border strips to match length. Sew borders to quilt sides.
2. Measure quilt from side to side and trim remaining border strips to match quilt width. Sew borders to top and bottom edges of quilt.

Quilting and Finishing

1. Mark quilting design on quilt top as desired. The quilt shown is outline-quilted with a stencil design quilted in muslin part of each block. A leaf and vine pattern is quilted in the borders.
2. Divide backing into two lengths. Cut one piece in half lengthwise. Join narrow panels to sides of wide piece to assemble backing.
3. Layer backing, batting, and quilt top. Baste. Quilt as desired.
4. Use remaining inner border fabric to make 9¾ yards of bias or straight-grain binding. See page 156 for instructions on making and applying binding.

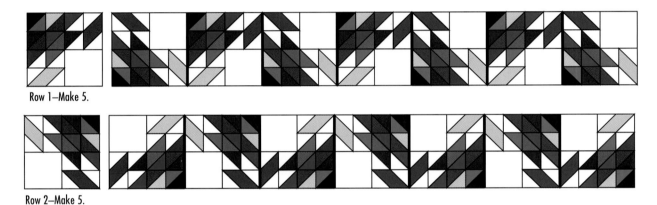

Row 1—Make 5.

Row 2—Make 5.

Row Assembly Diagram

Size Variations

	Twin	Queen/King
Finished Size	60" x 92"	92" x 92"
Number of Blocks	60	100
Blocks Set	6 x 10	10 x 10
Yardage Required		
¼-yard scraps	19	31
Muslin	4¾ yards	6¾ yards
Binding fabric	¾ yard	1 yard
Backing fabric	5½ yards	8¼ yards

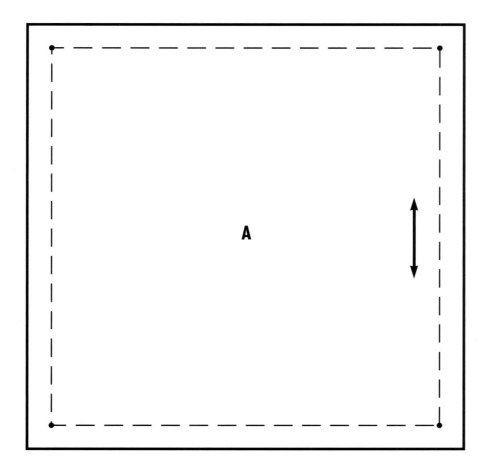

A

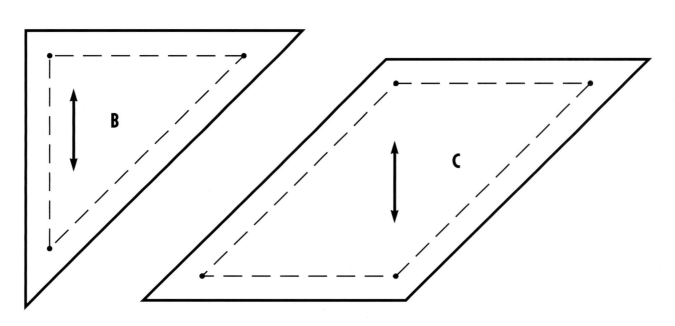

B

C

folk art freedom

When is a Log Cabin quilt anything but standard? When Terry Benzo dresses it up with borders of brick patchwork and appliquéd folk art motifs. This is a quilt that mixes tradition with fun new ideas, and a rich assortment of plaids and prints with the colors of hearth and home. Make your own version of this cozy quilt to cover you and yours with love.

Finished Size

Quilt: 62" x 67"
Blocks: 42 blocks, 5¼" x 5¼"
This quilt fits a twin-size bed. See Size Variations (page 107) for other size requirements.

Materials

18 (⅛-yard) pieces or equivalent scraps
2 (½-yard) pieces for bias appliqué
2 (¼-yard) pieces for bias appliqué
1¾ yards red fabric for patchwork, border, and binding
2¼ yards black fabric
4 yards backing fabric
72" x 90" precut batting
½"- and ¼"-wide pressing bars
Embroidery floss (optional)

Quilt by Terry Benzo of Pittsburgh, Pennsylvania

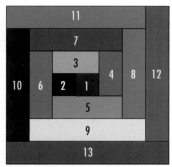

Log Cabin Block—Make 42.

Cutting

Instructions are for rotary cutting. Cut all strips cross-grain. Before making blocks, cut and set aside the pieces listed here so you can add the remaining fabric to your selection of scraps for piecing and appliqué.

1. For bias appliqué, cut an 18" square from each ½-yard piece and a 7" square from each ¼-yard piece.

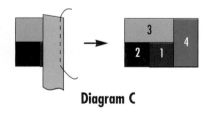

Diagram A

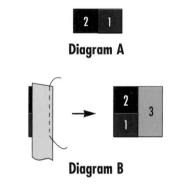

Diagram B

Diagram C

Diagram D

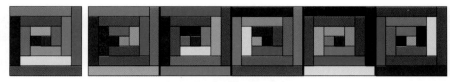

Row Assembly Diagram

2. From red fabric, cut four 3" x 54" lengthwise strips for middle border and one 30" square for binding.

3. From black fabric, cut four 6¼" x 66" lengthwise strips for outer border, four 1⅝" x 40" cross-grain strips for inner border, and one 17" x 40" lengthwise piece for brick border.

Making Blocks

For this stitch-and-cut method, it is not necessary to cut individual pieces for the logs.

1. Cut one 1¼"-wide strip from each scrap fabric. As you assemble blocks, cut more strips as needed.

2. To start first block, cut 1¼" squares from two strips. Join squares to form block center (Diagram A).

3. To sew first log, match one strip to longer edge of square pair, right sides facing, and stitch (Diagram B). Trim log even with bottom square. Press seam allowance toward log.

4. Turn block to position new log at top. With right sides facing, match another strip to right edge and stitch (Diagram C). Trim new log even with block as before, and press seam allowance toward log.

5. Turn unit so newest log is at top. With right sides facing, match another strip to right edge of block and stitch (Diagram D). Trim log even with block and press.

6. Continue adding logs in this manner until you have three logs on all sides of center square (see block diagram for numbered sequence of logs). Always press

seam allowances toward newest log. Completed block will measure approximately 5¾" square.

7. In this manner, make 42 Log Cabin blocks. Save remaining cut strips for second border.

Quilt Assembly

1. For each horizontal row, lay out six blocks as shown (Row Assembly Diagram). Lay out seven rows. Arrange blocks to get a pleasing balance of color and value, turning blocks as desired. When satisfied with placement, join blocks in each row.

2. Referring to photo on page 106, join rows.

Borders

1. Use 1⅝" x 40" black strips for first border. Referring to page 150, measure quilt from top to bottom and trim two border strips to match length. Sew borders to quilt sides.

2. Measure quilt from side to side, and trim remaining borders to match quilt width. Sew borders to top and bottom edges of quilt.

3. From remaining 1¼"-wide scrap strips, cut 90 (4"-long) pieces for second border. Join pieces end-to-end to make a continuous strip approximately 315" long.

4. Sew pieced strip to top edge of quilt; then trim strip even with quilt sides. Press seam allowances toward first border. Repeat to add second row of border at top edge. (Seams in pieced borders should offset by at least 1".) Add two border rows to bottom edge of quilt; then add side borders in same manner.

5. Use 17" x 40" black fabric to cut triangles A and C for brick border. From this fabric, cut one 6⅝" square and 31 (3⅞") squares. Cut each square in quarters diagonally to get four C triangles and 124 A triangles. (For traditional cutting, use patterns on page 107.)

6. From scrap fabrics, cut 64 (2⅜" x 4¼") B rectangles.

7. Select 29 A triangles, 15 B rectangles, and one C triangle for top border. Sew A triangles to both ends of 14 Bs as shown (Border Assembly Diagram). Join units in a row as shown. Sew remaining A triangle to last B piece, and join unit to right end of row. Sew C triangle to last B unit to complete row. Make border for bottom row in same manner. Make brick side borders in same manner, using 33 A triangles, 17 B rectangles, and one C triangle for each border.

8. Sew each border to quilt, easing to fit as needed. See page 151 for tips on mitering border corners.

9. Follow steps 1 and 2 to measure, trim, and sew middle and outer borders.

Border Assembly Diagram

piΠpoint∫

Buttonhole-Stitch Appliqué

Terry Benzo uses buttonhole stitch to secure appliqués and enhance the folk-art look of her work. Some sewing machines can make this decorative stitch, using regular sewing thread. However, most people work it by hand with floss or pearl cotton. Thread color can either match or contrast with the appliqué.

Buttonhole-stitch appliqué is particularly suitable for pieces applied with fusible web that don't have a turned edge—the stitch covers and camouflages the raw edge and prevents fraying. Look for more on fusible appliqué on page 81.

Thread needle with two or three strands of floss, knotted at end. Pull needle and thread up through base fabric (a). Reinsert needle through appliqué (b), ⅛" to ¼" from edge. Bring needle back up through base fabric just beyond edge and through thread loop (c) (Diagram 1).

Pull thread taut. Continue around appliqué piece, working same-size stitches from left to right (Diagram 2).

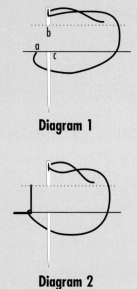

Diagram 1

Diagram 2

Appliqué

Appliqué patterns are on page 108. See page 156 for instructions on making continuous bias and page 134 got tips on bias appliqué. See page 149 for information on cutting and preparing pieces for hand appliqué.

1. From one 18" square, make 6 yards of 1½"-wide continuous bias. From this, cut two 3-yard-long strips for appliqué.

2. Fold, stitch, and press bias strip with ½"-wide pressing bar.

3. Fold bias strip in half to find center. Pin center of vine at mitered seam. Referring to photo on page 106, pin vine in place on borders, letting it curl up and down in random curves or as desired. Repeat vine placement at opposite corner.

4. Cut pieces for two birds from scrap fabrics; prepare pieces for appliqué. Referring to photo, pin birds in place at border corners.

5. From remaining 18" square, cut 6 yards of 1"-wide continuous bias. Fold, stitch, and press bias strips with ¼"-wide pressing bar. (Trim seam allowance on stitched strip as necessary.) Cut bias into strips of varying lengths from 10" to 18" long. Hiding ends under first vine, pin narrow stems in place, curving stems as desired.

6. From each 7" square, make 1 yard of ¼"-wide vines in same manner. Pin stems in place on previous vines as desired.

7. From scraps, cut an assortment of hearts, leaves, and flowers. Pin hearts and flowers at ends of each vine and stem. Place leaves on vine randomly as shown.

8. Adjust vine and appliqués to achieve a pleasing arrangement. Reposition vines or experiment with placement of shapes and assortment of fabrics. When satisfied with placement, appliqué all pieces in place. Use traditional appliqué methods or see page 105 for PinPoints on buttonhole-stitch appliqué.

Quilting and Finishing

1. Mark quilting design on quilt top as desired. Quilt shown has crosshatching and outline quilting in the borders and an allover clamshell design in the blocks.

2. Divide backing into two equal lengths. Cut one piece in half lengthwise. Join a narrow panel to each side of wide piece to assemble backing.

3. Layer backing, batting, and quilt top. Backing seams will parallel top and bottom edges of quilt. Baste. Quilt as desired.

4. Make 7½ yards of bias or straight-grain binding. See page 156 for instructions on making and applying binding.

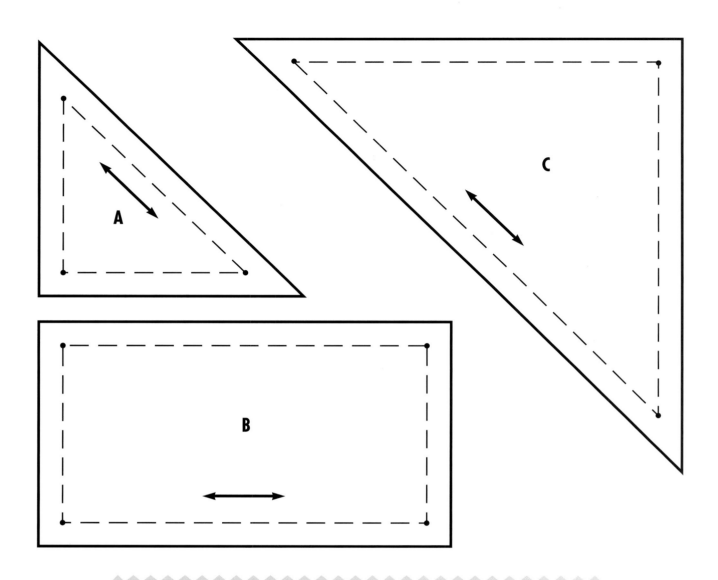

Size Variations

	Full	Queen	King
Finished Size	77½" x 88"	88" x 88"	98½" x 98½"
Number of Blocks	99	121	169
Blocks Set	9 x 11	11 x 11	13 x 13
Number of			
A triangles	144	196	228
B rectangles	74	100	116
Yardage Required			
⅛-yard pieces	43	52	73
Bias appliqué			
Large vines	2 (⅝-yard) pieces	2 (¾-yard) pieces	2 (¾-yard) pieces
Small vines	2 (⅜-yard) pieces	2 (¾-yard) pieces	2 (¾-yard) pieces
Red fabric	2¼ yards	2½ yards	2⅝ yards
Black fabric	2½ yards	2¾ yards	3 yards
Backing fabric	5½ yards (108" wide)	8¼ yards	3 yards

string squares

Waste not, want not, as the saying goes. String piecing can be a scrap saver's favorite technique because it helps a quilt-maker use up the narrowest of leftover fabrics. Join strips to create new "fabric" from which pieces are cut. This quilt uses different fabrics and strip widths to get a terrific look. The muted colors are an autumn harvest of pumpkin, cinnamon, maple leaf red, and goldenrod. A mix of print and plaid fabrics balances light, medium, and dark values.

Finished Size

Quilt: 65" x 77"
Blocks: 20 blocks, 12¼" x 12¼"
This quilt fits a twin-size bed.
See Size Variations (page 112) for other size requirements.

Materials

14 fat quarters (18" x 22" pieces)
    or equivalent scraps
¾ yard fabric for inner border
2 yards fabric for outer border
⅞ yard binding fabric
4 yards backing fabric
72" x 90" precut batting

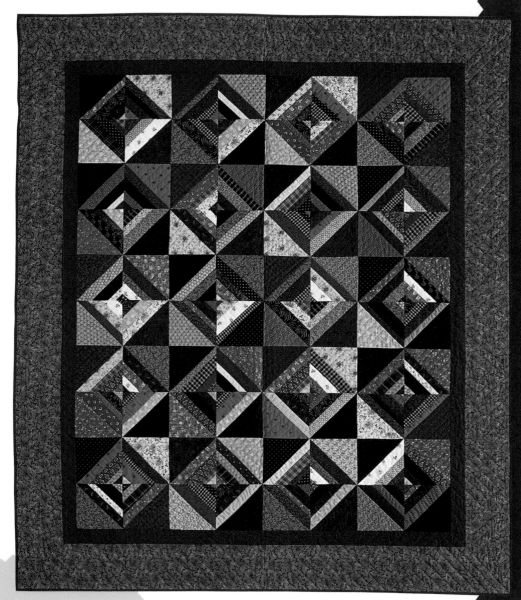

Quilt by Carole Collins of Norfolk, Nebraska

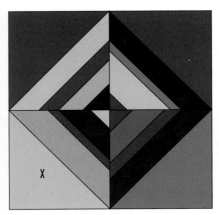

String Squares Block—Make 20.

Quarter-Block Unit—Make 80.

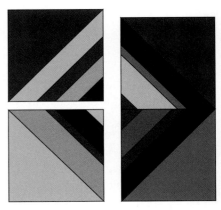

Block Assembly Diagram

Making Blocks

Instructions are for rotary cutting. Cut all strips cross-grain. For traditional cutting, use pattern on page 112.

1. From fabric for outer border, cut four 6½"-wide lengthwise strips. Set these aside for border. Add remaining fabric to scraps.

2. From scraps, cut 40 (7") squares. Cut each square in half diagonally to get 80 X triangles. Set triangles aside.

3. From remaining fabrics, cut 27 strips about 21" long in four strip widths: 1¼" wide, 1½" wide, 1¾" wide, and 2" wide. Cut a total of 108 strips. (*Note:* It's a good idea to cut some strips on the bias. When string-pieced triangles are cut from strip sets, most cut edges will be bias. But if the original cut strip is bias, then cut edge will be straight grain. Mixing grain direction will reduce danger of distortion when working with string-pieced triangles.)

4. Select one strip of each width. Join these four strips lengthwise—in any order—to make a strip set. Width of assembled strip set should be 5". (*Note:* If you use more strips or strips of different widths, make sure finished strip set is 5" wide, including seam allowances at outside edges.) Make 27 strip sets, each a different combination of fabrics. Press seam allowances in each strip set in same direction.

5. Using acrylic ruler, align 45°-angle marking with bottom of one strip set to establish a 45° angle. Rotary-cut three X triangles from strip set as shown (**Cutting Diagram**). Repeat with remaining strip set to get a total of 80 string-pieced triangles.

6. Join each string-pieced triangle with a solid triangle to get a quarter-block unit. Make 80 units as shown. On 40 units, press seam allowances toward solid triangle; on remaining units, press toward pieced triangle.

7. Select four quarter-block units for each block. Join blocks in pairs (**Block Assembly Diagram**). Then join pairs to complete block.

8. Make 20 blocks.

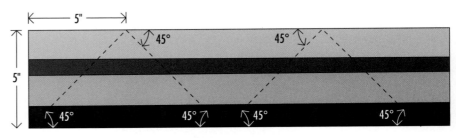

Cutting Diagram

Quilt Assembly

1. For each horizontal row, lay out four blocks as shown **(Row Assembly Diagram)**. Lay out five rows. Arrange blocks to get a pleasing balance of color and value. When satisfied with placement, join blocks in each row.
2. Referring to photo on page 109, join rows.

Borders

1. From inner border fabric, cut eight 2½"-wide crosswise strips. Join two strips end-to-end to make each border.
2. Referring to page 150, measure quilt from top to bottom and trim side borders to match length. Sew borders to quilt sides.
3. Measure quilt from side to side and trim remaining borders to match quilt width. Sew borders to top and bottom edges of quilt.
4. Repeat steps 2 and 3 to sew outer border to quilt.

Quilting and Finishing

1. Mark quilting design on quilt top as desired. Quilt shown is outline-quilted.
2. Divide backing into two equal lengths. Cut one piece in half lengthwise. Join a narrow panel to each side of wide piece to assemble backing.
3. Layer backing, batting, and quilt top. Backing seams will parallel top and bottom edges of quilt. Baste. Quilt as desired.
4. Make 8¼ yards of bias or straight-grain binding. See page 156 for instructions on making and applying binding.

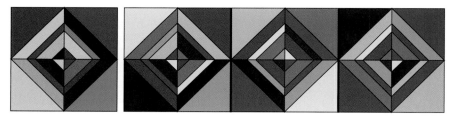

Row Assembly Diagram

A Quilt for All Seasons
Carole Collins's quilt uses the colors of autumn. Here are suggestions for *String Squares* in color schemes for winter, spring, and summer.

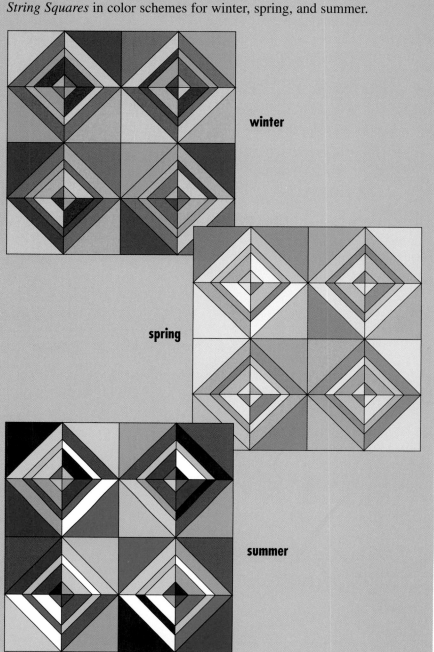

winter

spring

summer

Size Variations

	Full	**Queen**	**King**
Finished Size	77" x 89½"	89½" x 102"	102" x 102"
Number of Blocks	30	42	49
Blocks Set	5 x 6	6 x 7	7 x 7
Yardage Required			
Fat quarters	22	30	37
Inner border fabric	¾ yard	¾ yard	¾ yard
Outer border fabric	2¼ yards	2⅝ yards	3 yards
Binding fabric	⅞ yard	⅞ yard	1 yard
Backing fabric	5½ yards	8¼ yards	9½ yards

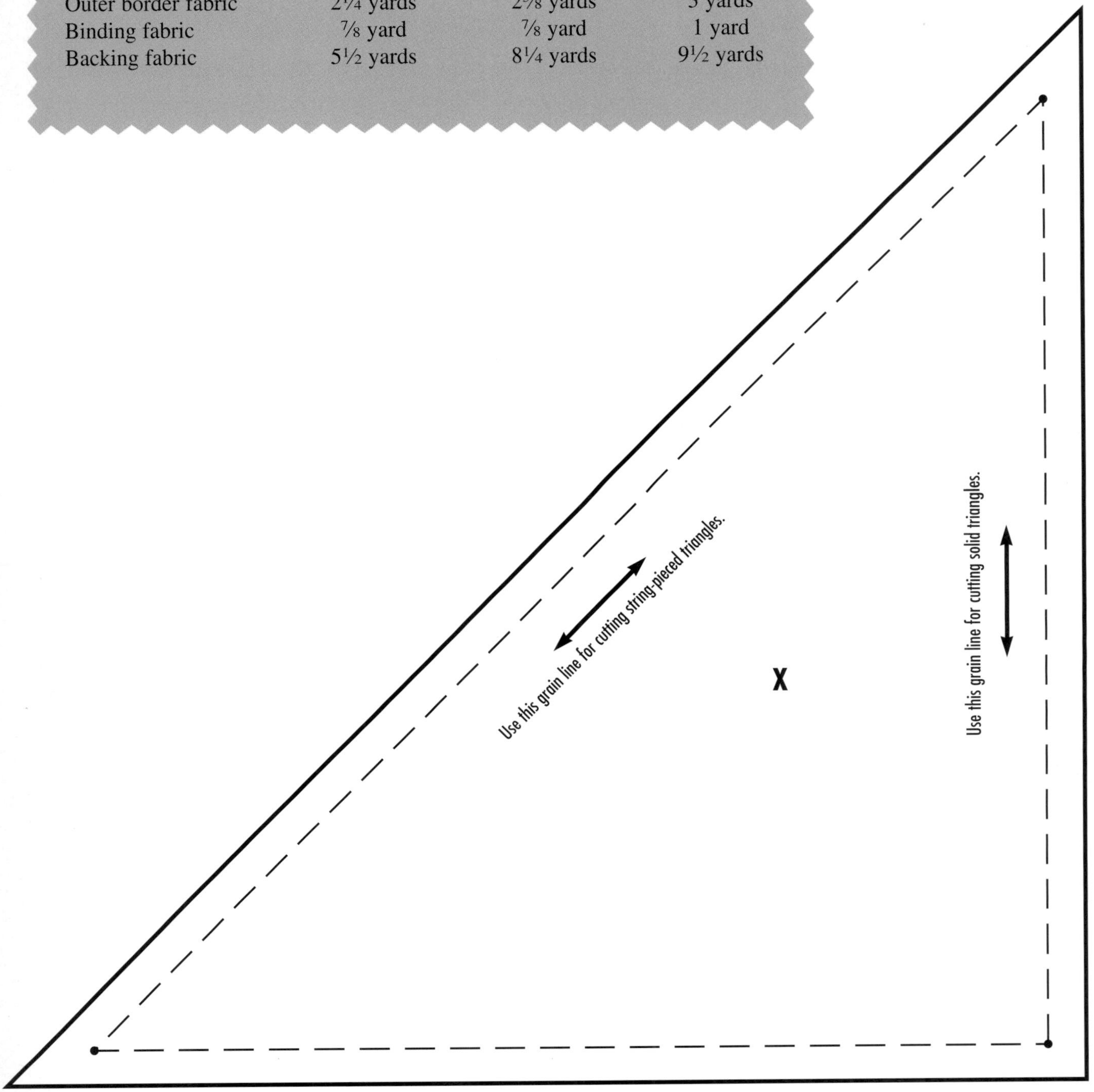

Use this grain line for cutting string-pieced triangles.

X

Use this grain line for cutting solid triangles.

railroad crossing

This modern-day interpretation of a nineteenth-century quilt captures the excitement of old Amish quilts with the simplicity of bright, solid colors against a dark background. Quick-piecing techniques are a bonus. Put your own stamp on this classic quilt by mixing prints with solids. Or turn the tables and make a soft, pastel version.

Finished Size

Quilt: 70" x 90"
Blocks: 12 blocks, 17" x 17"
This quilt fits a twin-size bed. See Size Variations (page 115) for other size requirements.

Materials

60 (7" x 17") solid-color fabrics
5⅜ yards black fabric (includes binding)
1 yard pale blue fabric for stars and inner border
5½ yards backing fabric
81" x 96" precut batting

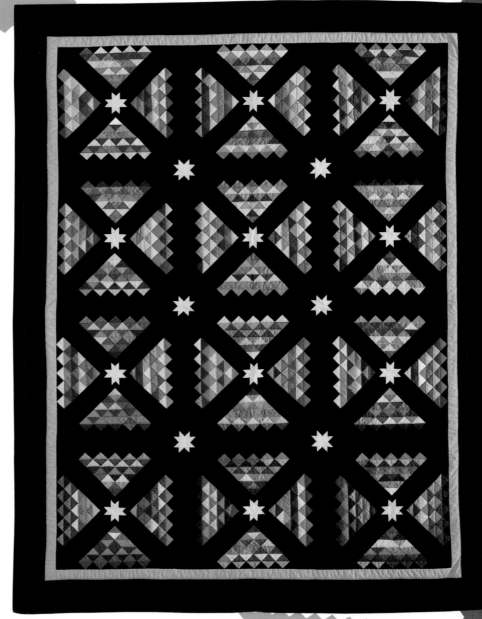

Quilt by Winnie S. Fleming of Houston, Texas; hand-quilted by Evelyn Anthony

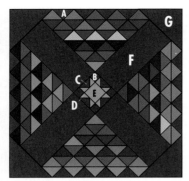

Railroad Crossing Block—Make 12.

Making Blocks

Instructions are for rotary cutting and quick piecing. Before cutting, read block instructions and decide whether you prefer quick piecing or traditional piecing. For traditional cutting, use patterns on page 116.

1. On wrong side of a light scrap fabric, draw a two-square by six-square grid of $2\frac{3}{8}$" squares (Diagram A). Mark diagonal lines through squares as shown.

2. Match marked fabric piece with a medium/dark fabric, right sides facing. Starting at middle of one side, stitch on both sides of diagonal lines, pivoting at grid corners as shown. (Blue line in diagram shows one continuous stitching line; red shows second stitching line.) Press stitching. Cut on all drawn lines to get 24 triangle-squares from grid. Stitch 30 grids to get a total of 720 triangle-squares. Press seam allowances toward darker fabric.

3. From black fabric, cut three $3\frac{3}{8}$"-wide cross-grain strips. From these, cut 48 ($3\frac{3}{8}$") squares. Cut each square in quarters diagonally to get 192 A triangles.

4. Each block has four quadrants of triangle-squares. For efficiency and to keep fabric placement random, make all the quadrants before assembling the blocks. For each quadrant, choose 15 triangle-squares and four A triangles. You can select the triangle-squares

Diagram A

$2\frac{3}{8}$"

Diagram B

Diagram C

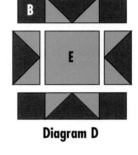

Diagram D

randomly, but the quilt shown has matching (more or less) triangle-squares in rows across the quadrant (see photo). Join A triangles and triangle-squares in rows as shown (Diagram B); then join rows to complete quadrant. Make 48 quadrants and set aside.

5. For stars, cut six $1\frac{1}{4}$"-wide cross-grain black strips and five same-size blue strips. From black strips, cut 72 ($1\frac{1}{4}$" x 2") Cs and 72 ($1\frac{1}{4}$") B squares. From blue strips, cut 144 ($1\frac{1}{4}$") D squares. From one 2"-wide blue strip, cut 18 (2") E squares.

6. Referring to page 146, use the diagonal-corner technique to sew two D squares to each C (Diagram C). Or sew D triangles to C traditionally as shown. Make four C/D units for each star, a total of 72. Press seams toward Ds.

7. For each star, select four Bs, four C/D units, and one E square. Join

units in rows as shown (Diagram D). Press seam allowances away from C/D units. Join rows to complete star. Make 18 star units, 12 for blocks and six for sashing.

8. From black fabric, cut three $5\frac{1}{8}$"-wide cross-grain strips and 17 ($3\frac{1}{2}$"-wide) strips. From wider strips, cut 24 ($5\frac{1}{8}$") squares. Cut each square in half diagonally to get 48 G triangles. From $3\frac{1}{2}$"-wide strips, cut 17 ($17\frac{1}{2}$"-long) strips for sashing and 48 (8"-long) F strips.

9. For each block, select one star unit and four each of F, G, and triangle-square quadrants. Join quadrants to sides of two F strips as shown (Block Assembly Diagram). Join remaining Fs to opposite sides of star. Press seam allowances toward Fs. Join three sections; then add G triangles to corners to complete block.

10. Make 12 blocks.

Block Assembly Diagram

Quilt Assembly

1. Lay out blocks in four horizontal rows with three blocks in each row (**Row Assembly Diagram**), placing a sashing strip between blocks. Arrange blocks to achieve a nice balance of color and value.
2. When satisfied with placement, join blocks in each row.
3. For sashing row, join three sashing strips and two star units as shown. Make three sashing rows.
4. Join rows, alternating block rows and sashing rows.

Borders

1. From remaining blue fabric, cut eight 2"-wide cross-grain strips. Join two strips end-to-end to make each border strip.
2. Referring to page 150, measure quilt from top to bottom and trim two borders to match length. Sew borders to quilt sides.
3. Measure quilt from side to side and trim remaining borders to match quilt width. Sew borders to top and bottom edges of quilt.

Block Row—Make 4.

Sashing Row—Make 3.

Row Assembly Diagram

4. From remaining black fabric, cut four 5¼" x 86" lengthwise strips. Repeat steps 2 and 3 to measure quilt, trim borders to fit, and sew borders to quilt.

Quilting and Finishing

1. Mark quilting design on quilt top as desired. Quilt shown has outline quilting in the blocks and a simple cable quilted in the sashing and borders.

2. Divide backing into two equal lengths. Cut one piece in half lengthwise. Join narrow panels to sides of wide piece to assemble backing.
3. Layer backing, batting, and quilt top. Baste. Quilt as desired.
4. Use remaining black fabric to make 9¼ yards of bias or straight-grain binding. See page 156 for instructions on making and applying binding.

	Queen	King
Size Variations*		
Finished Size	90" x 90"	110" x 110"
Number of Blocks	16	25
Blocks Set	4 x 4	5 x 5
Number of		
Sashing Strips	24	40
Stars	25	41
Yardage Required		
7" x 17" scraps	80	126
Blue fabric	1 yard	1⅜ yards
Black fabric	6½ yards	9¼ yards
Backing fabric	2¾ yards	3¼ yards
	(108" wide)	(120" wide)

Note: The size of this block makes a full-size variation impractical.

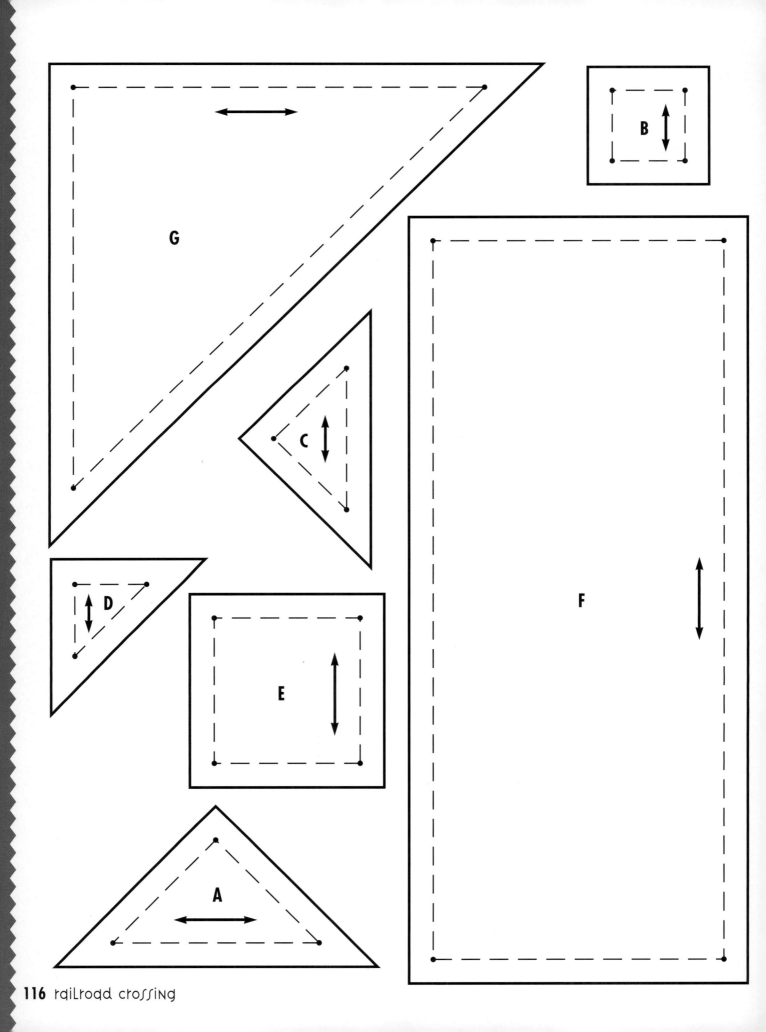

The nineteenth-century quiltmaker who made this charming quilt didn't have the benefit of an acrylic ruler, with neatly marked 60° angles to guide her cutting. To follow in her footsteps, you can use traditional cutting and sewing methods, or you can rotary-cut and strip-piece with today's handy tools and techniques. Either way, you'll make a quilt to be proud of.

Finished Size

Quilt: 60" x 78½"
Blocks: 28 blocks, 9¾" x 11¼"
This quilt fits a twin-size bed. See Size Variations (page 119) for other size requirements.

Materials

10 fat quarters (18" x 22" pieces)
    blue fabrics or equivalent scraps
5 fat quarters (18" x 22" pieces)
    white fabrics or equivalent scraps
½ yard tan fabric
⅛ yard red fabric
3 yards tone-on-tone pink fabric
¾ yard inner border fabric
¾ yard binding fabric
3¾ yards backing fabric
72" x 90" precut batting

Antique quilt owned by Patricia Cox of Minneapolis, Minnesota

Starburst Block—Make 28.

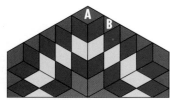

Half-Block—Make 4.

Making Blocks

Instructions are for rotary cutting and quick piecing. Before cutting, read block instructions and decide whether you prefer quick piecing or traditional piecing. For traditional cutting, use patterns on page 122.

1. Cut blue, white, tan, and red fabrics into 1½" x 18" strips. For strip sets, cut 135 blue strips, 68 white strips, 20 tan strips, and three red strips.

2. Referring to **Strip Set Diagrams**, join blue and white strips to make 22 of Strip Set 1 and 23 of Strip Set 2. Make 20 of Strip Set 3 as shown with tan fabric and three of Strip Set 3 with red fabric. Press all seam allowances toward blue fabric. (Set aside remaining blue strips for A diamonds.)

3. Place one strip set on cutting mat. Position ruler with one 60° marking aligned with bottom edge of strip set as shown (**Diagram A**). Make this first cut to remove selvage and establish a 60° angle.

4. Turn the strip set or the mat to position the cut edge to your left. Position ruler with the line marking 1½" on the cut edge; then

cut a 1½"-wide diagonal strip (**Diagram B**). Cut eight 1½"-wide segments from each strip set, keeping separate stacks of segments from sets 1, 2, and 3.

5. Cut 14 (1¾"-wide) cross-grain strips of pink fabric. From these, cut 544 B triangles. To rotary-cut triangles, start in same manner as for strip sets, aligning one 60° marking with

bottom of strip to make first cut (**Diagram C**). To make second cut, align second 60° marking with bottom of strip and edge of ruler with top corner of strip (**Diagram D**). To cut next triangle, realign ruler to first 60° marking (**Diagram E**). Continue cutting triangles, alternating alignment of ruler with each cut.

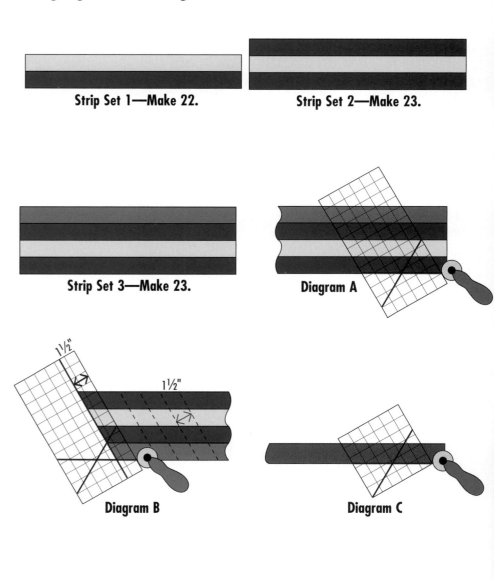

Strip Set 1—Make 22.

Strip Set 2—Make 23.

Strip Set 3—Make 23.

Diagram A

Diagram B

Diagram C

Diagram D

Diagram E

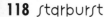

6. Sew a B triangle to bottom of each segment of strip sets 1 and 2 (Diagram F).

7. Use technique for cutting strip sets to rotary-cut 184 A diamonds from remaining blue strips. Sew Bs to one edge of each blue A diamond (Diagram F).

8. For one block, select six A/B units and six segments *each* of strip sets 1, 2, and 3. (Units from Strip Set 3 should have same contrasting fabric for center star, but remaining units can vary if you want to mix blue fabrics.) Join units as shown to make six block sections (Diagram F). Press seam allowances toward strip set segments 1 and 3.

9. Join six sections in groups of three; then join block halves as shown (Block Assembly Diagram).

10. Set aside a 14" x 76" lengthwise strip of pink fabric for borders. From remaining 28"-wide piece, cut 12 (1½"-wide) strips. From these, cut 180 A diamonds (six for each block). Set-in pink diamonds at corners to complete

block. (See page 14 for tips on sewing a set-in seam.)

11. For half-block, make two sections and two partial sections as shown (Half-Block Assembly Diagram). Partial sections consist of one Strip Set 1 segment, one Strip Set 3 segment, and 2 extra B triangles. Join sections and set-in three A diamonds to complete half-block. Dotted line in diagram indicates seam line for quilt assembly; excess fabric will then be trimmed from seam allowance.

12. Make 28 Starburst blocks and four half-blocks.

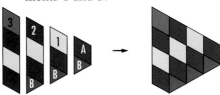

Diagram F

Block Assembly Diagram

Half-Block Assembly Diagram

Size Variations

	Full/Queen	King
Finished Size	80" x 101"	99" x 101"
Number of Blocks	53	68
Half Blocks	6	8
Strip Set 1	42	53
Strip Set 2	43	55
Strip Set 3	43	55
Blocks Set	7 x 8	9 x 8
Number of Pieces to Cut		
Blue A	330	424
Pink A	336	432
Pink B	1,014	1,304
Pink C	104	134
Pink D	16	20
Yardage Required		
Blue fat quarters	18	23
White fat quarters	10	12
Tan fat quarters	3	4
Red fat quarters	1	1
Pink fabric	4½ yards	5⅝ yards
Inner border fabric	¾ yard	1⅛ yards
Binding fabric	¾ yard	⅞ yard
108"-wide backing fabric	2½ yards	3 yards

Quilt Assembly

1. From remaining pink fabric, cut seven 5⅝" x 28" strips. From these, use rotary-cutting technique described on page 188, Step 5, to cut 54 C triangles.

2. From one 6⅛"-wide pink strip, cut six 3⅝" x 6⅛" rectangles. Cut three rectangles in half diagonally in one direction to get six D triangles (Diagram G). Cut remaining rectangles in half in other direction to get six Ds reversed (Diagram G). Referring to pattern on page 122, trim ¾" from tip of each triangle.

3. For Row 1, lay out six blocks in a vertical row, with a pink A diamond at the top of each block. Fill spaces between blocks with Cs (Row Assembly Diagram). Sew Ds and Ds reversed to first and last blocks in the row as shown. When satisfied with position of blocks, sew Cs to opposite edges of each block. Press seam allowances toward triangles. Join block/triangle units to complete row. Make three of Row 1.

4. For Row 2, lay out five blocks and two half-blocks, placing Cs between blocks as shown. Sew Cs to each block; then join block/triangle units to complete row. Make two of Row 2.

5. Referring to assembly diagram and photo on page 121, join rows.

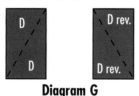

Diagram G

Borders

1. Cut eight 3"-wide cross-grain strips for inner border. Sew two strips end-to-end to make a border strip for each quilt side.

2. Referring to page 150, measure quilt from top to bottom and trim two borders to match length. Sew borders to quilt sides.

Row Assembly Diagram

3. Measure quilt from side to side and trim remaining borders to match quilt width. Sew borders to top and bottom edges of quilt.

4. For outer border, cut four 3½"-wide lengthwise strips from reserved fabric. Measure quilt length and trim two strips to match as before. Sew borders to quilt sides. Measure quilt width and trim remaining strips to match; sew borders to top and bottom edges of quilt.

Quilting and Finishing

1. Mark quilting design on quilt top as desired. The quilt shown has diagonal lines, spaced ½" apart, quilted across the quilt surface.

2. Divide backing into two equal lengths. Cut one piece in half lengthwise. Join a narrow panel to each side of wide piece to assemble backing.

3. Layer backing, batting, and quilt top. Backing seams will parallel top and bottom edges of quilt. Baste. Quilt as desired.

4. Make 8 yards of bias or straight-grain binding. See page 156 for instructions on making and applying binding.

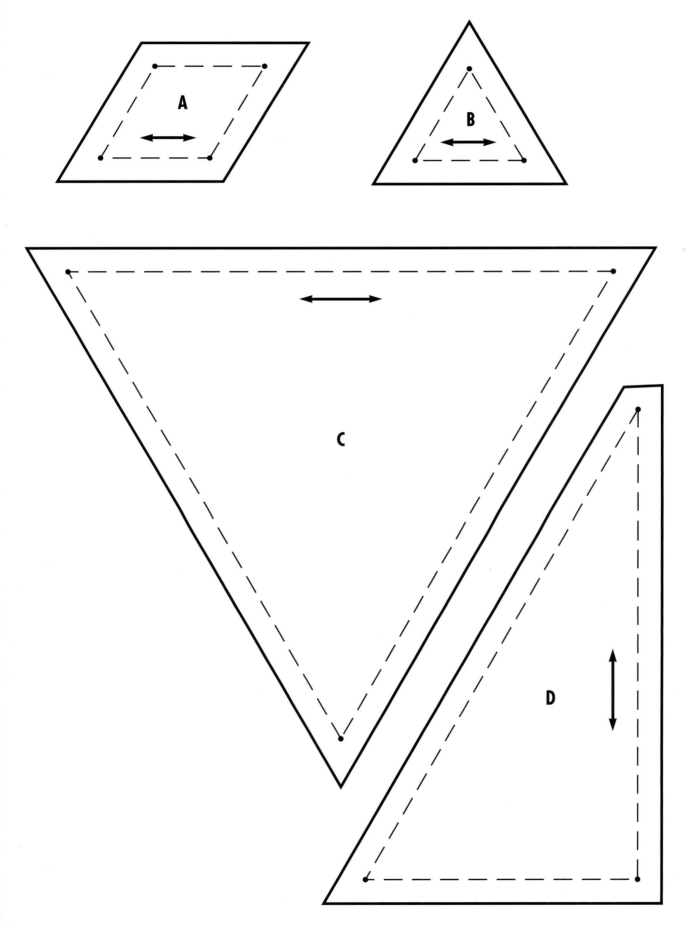

A

B

C

D

bear's paw

Quick piecing makes triangle-squares easy to sew, and this quilt has lots of them, including an eye-catching sawtooth border. The Bear's Paw block has many variations and names, including Duck's Foot in the Mud, Hand of Friendship, Cat's Paw, Small Hand, and Illinois Turkey Track.

Finished Size

Quilt: 67" x 83"
Blocks: 12 blocks, 14" x 14"
This quilt fits a twin-size bed. See Size Variations (page125) for other size requirements.

Materials

6 (12½" x 18") green prints
6 (12½" x 18") red prints
13 (12½" x 18") tone-on-tone background prints
12½" x 18" green solid fabric
1½ yards red solid fabric (includes binding)
2¼ yards print fabric
5 yards backing fabric
72" x 90" precut batting

Quilt by Winnie S. Fleming of Houston, Texas

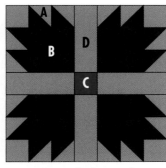

Bear's Paw Block—Make 12.

Making Blocks

Instructions are for rotary cutting and quick piecing. Before cutting, read block instructions and decide whether you prefer quick piecing or traditional piecing. For traditional cutting, use patterns on page 126.

1. Cut a 7½" x 18" piece for triangle-squares from each 12½" x 18" piece of red print, green print, background print, and green solid.

2. On wrong side of each background piece, draw a two-square by six-square grid of 2⅞" squares **(Diagram A)**. Mark diagonal lines through centers of squares as shown.

3. Match a marked piece with a red or green piece, right sides facing. Starting at middle of one side, stitch on both sides of diagonal lines, pivoting at grid corners as shown. (Red line in diagram indicates one continuous stitching line; blue line is second continuous line.) Press stitching. Cut on all drawn lines to get 24 triangle-squares from each grid. Stitch 13 grids to get a total of 312 triangle-squares. Press seam allowances toward dark fabric.

4. Find 16 matching triangle-squares for each block. (Set 120 triangle-squares aside for border.) For each block, use matching scrap of background fabric to cut four 2½" C squares and four 2½" x 6½" Ds. From matching print fabric, cut four 4½" B squares.

5. Cut nine 2½" C squares from remaining solid green fabric. From red solid fabric, cut eight 2½"-wide crosswise strips for middle border. From ends of these strips, cut nine 2½" C squares. Set aside three Cs of each color for sashing. Match remaining squares with pieces for each block as desired.

6. For each block, join triangle-squares in eight pairs as shown, always sewing print fabric to background fabric **(Block Assembly Diagram)**. Sew one pair to a B square as shown. Join C background square to remaining pair; then join three-square strip to adjacent side of B. Press seam allowances toward B. Make four units in this manner.

7. Join two units to opposite sides of two D pieces as shown. Press seam allowances toward D.

8. Sew remaining Ds to opposite sides of solid-colored C square. Press seam allowances toward Ds.

9. Join rows to complete block. Make 12 blocks.

Quilt Assembly

1. Alternating red and green blocks, lay out blocks in four horizontal rows with three blocks in each row **(Row Assembly Diagram)**. Arrange blocks to achieve a pleasing balance of color and value.

2. When satisfied with placement, join blocks in each row.

3. For sashing row, join three sashing strips and two sashing squares as shown. Make three sashing rows, placing red and green sashing squares as desired.

4. Join rows as shown in photo, alternating block rows and sashing rows.

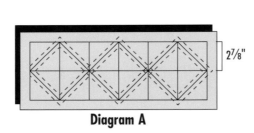

Diagram A

2⅞"

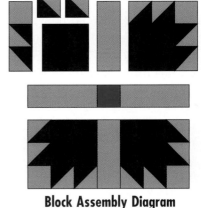

Block Assembly Diagram

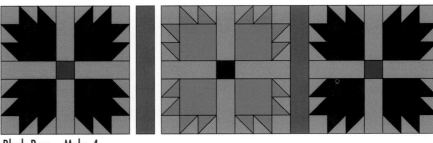

Block Row—Make 4.

Sashing Row—Make 3.

Row Assembly Diagram

Borders

1. From print border fabric, cut four 2½" x 65" lengthwise strips. Referring to page 150, measure quilt from top to bottom; trim two borders to match length. Sew borders to quilt sides.
2. Measure quilt from side to side and trim remaining borders to match quilt width. Sew borders to top and bottom edges of quilt.
3. Join two red strips end-to-end for each middle border. Repeat steps 1 and 2 to measure the quilt, trim borders to fit, and sew borders to edges of quilt.
4. From scraps, cut two 2⅞" squares each of background fabric and print border fabric. Cut squares in half to get four A triangles. Join a background triangles to print triangle to get four triangle-squares, bringing total for sawtooth border to 124 triangle-squares.
5. Select 34 triangle-squares for one side border. Join squares in a vertical row, sewing background fabric triangle to print triangle and changing direction in middle of row as shown (see photo). Sew border to one side of quilt, easing as necessary. Repeat for second side border.
6. For top border, join 26 triangle-squares in a horizontal row, again changing direction in middle of row as shown. Add one square to each end of row, changing position of end squares as shown in photo. Sew row to top edge of quilt, easing as needed. Repeat for bottom border.
7. For the outer border, cut four 5"-wide lengthwise strips from print fabric. Measure the quilt. Trim and sew outer borders to quilt as for inner borders.

Quilting and Finishing

1. Mark quilting design on quilt top as desired. Quilt shown has diagonal lines quilted in the blocks and borders.
2. Divide backing into two lengths. Cut one piece in half lengthwise. Join a narrow panel to each side of wide piece to make backing.
3. Layer backing, batting, and quilt top. Baste. Quilt as desired.
4. Use remaining red solid fabric to make 9 yards of bias or straight-grain binding. See page 156 for instructions on making and applying binding.

Size Variations

	Full/Queen	King
Finished Size	83" x 99"	99" x 99"
Number of Blocks	20	25
Blocks Set	4 x 5	5 x 5
Number of		
Sashing Strips	31	40
Sashing Squares	12	16
Triangle-Squares for Border	160	176
Yardage Required		
Green prints	10	13
Red prints	10	12
Background prints	20	25
Green solid fabric	10 (2½") squares	12 (2½") squares
Red solid fabric	1½ yards	1½ yards
Print border fabric	2⅝ yards	2⅞ yards
108"-wide backing fabric	2½ yards	3 yards

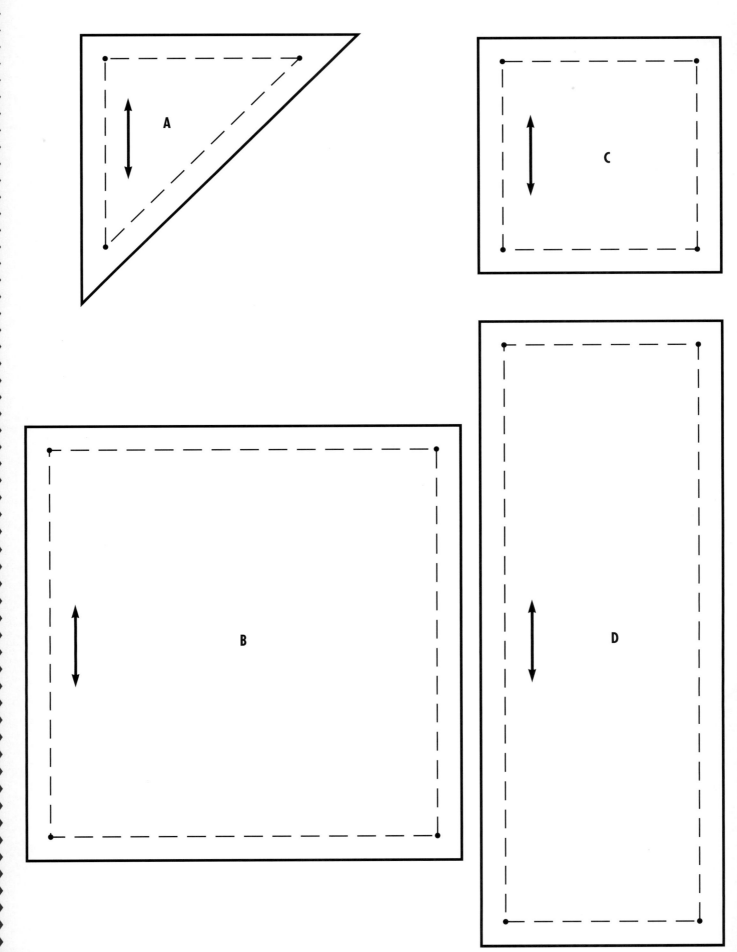

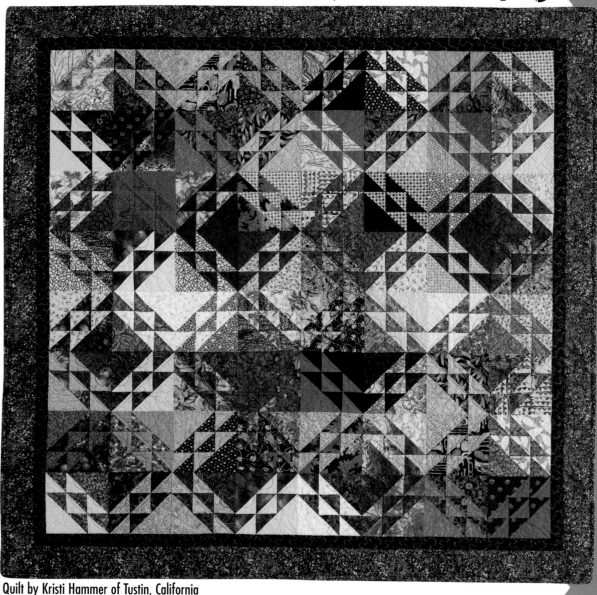

Quilt by Kristi Hammer of Tustin, California

Kristi Hammer updates an easy-to-sew block of triangles by adding scraps to the recipe. Instead of using one fabric in each block, she places a different fabric of the same color family in each quadrant of the block. The interplay of light, medium, and dark fabrics makes this quilt a shimmering interpretation of a time-honored favorite.

Finished Size

Quilt: 56" x 56"
Blocks: 16 blocks, 12" x 12"
This quilt is a wall hanging or lap-size quilt. See Size Variations (page 129) for other size requirements.

Materials

32 (6" x 14") light/medium fabrics or equivalent scraps
32 (6" x 14") medium/dark fabrics or equivalent scraps*
⅜ yard fabric for inner border
1¾ yards fabric for outer border and binding
3⅜ yards backing fabric
72" x 90" precut batting
Note: Divide fabrics into eight color groups, with four fabrics in each group.

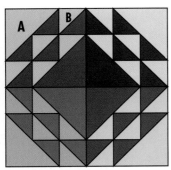

Corn & Beans Block—Make 16.

Making Blocks

Instructions are for rotary cutting. For traditional cutting, use patterns on page 130.

1. From each scrap fabric, cut one $4\frac{7}{8}$" square and five $2\frac{7}{8}$" squares. Cut large square in half diagonally to get two A triangles. Cut smaller squares in half diagonally to get 10 B triangles. Divide triangles into two equal sets, one for each of two blocks.

2. For each block, select four sets of medium/dark triangles from the same color family. Pair each dark set with a light/medium set. (Treat mediums as either light or dark, depending on the value of its companion fabric.) Each pair of fabrics makes one quadrant of a block.

3. To assemble block, work on one quadrant at a time. Begin with B triangles. First join three light/dark pairs into triangle-squares as shown in top left corner of **Block Assembly Diagram**. Press seam allowances toward dark fabric.

4. Join remaining B triangles to triangle-squares, making three horizontal rows as shown (bottom left corner of diagram). Join rows to complete center section of quadrant (bottom right corner of diagram).

5. Sew light and dark A triangles to opposite sides of unit as shown.

6. Repeat steps 3–5 to complete four quadrants for each block.

7. Position quadrants as shown, with light A triangles at outside corners. Join adjacent units to make two halves of block. Press seam allowances in opposite directions. Join halves to complete block.

8. Make 16 blocks in this manner.

Quilt Assembly

1. Lay out blocks in four horizontal rows of four blocks each. Arrange blocks to get a pleasing balance of color and value. When satisfied with placement, join blocks in each row (**Row Assembly Diagram**).

2. Referring to photo, join rows.

Borders

1. For the inner border, cut eight $1\frac{1}{2}$"-wide cross-grain strips. Join two strips end-to-end for each border.

2. Referring to page 150, measure quilt from top to bottom and trim two borders to match length. Sew borders to quilt sides.

3. Measure quilt from side to side and trim remaining borders to match quilt width. Sew borders to top and bottom edges of quilt.

4. For outer border, cut four $3\frac{1}{2}$"-wide lengthwise strips. Measure quilt; then trim and sew borders to quilt as for inner border.

Quilting and Finishing

1. Mark quilting design on quilt top as desired. Quilt shown is machine-quilted in an allover pattern, with a leaf border design.

2. Divide backing into two equal lengths. Cut one piece in half lengthwise. Sew a narrow panel to one side of wide piece. Discard remaining narrow panel.

3. Layer backing, batting, and quilt top. Baste. Quilt as desired.

4. Use remaining border fabric to make $6\frac{1}{2}$ yards of bias or straight-grain binding. See page 156 for instructions on making and applying binding.

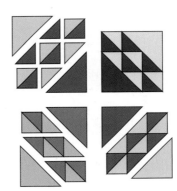

Block Assembly Diagram

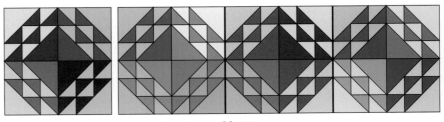

Row Assembly Diagram

Size Variations

	Twin	Full	Queen	King
Finished Size	68" x 92"	80" x 92"	92" x 104"	104" x 104"
Number of Blocks	35	42	56	64
Blocks Set	5 x 7	6 x 7	7 x 8	8 x 8
Yardage Required				
Dark scraps	18	21	28	32
Light scraps	18	21	28	32
Inner border fabric	½ yard	½ yard	½ yard	½ yard
Outer border fabric	2⅝ yards	2⅝ yards	3 yards	3 yards
Backing fabric	5¾ yards	5¾ yards	8½ yards	9½ yards

Color Choices

If the earthtones of Kristi's quilt are not your style, just imagine a color scheme that suits you. To give you some ideas, we've illustrated a few suggestions. The sky's the limit!

Black & White

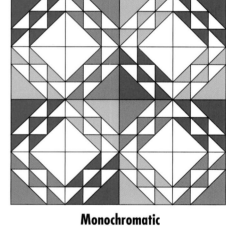

Monochromatic

Amish Traditions

Sea & Sky

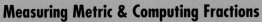

Measuring Metric & Computing Fractions

If you are accustomed to the metric system, this chart will be helpful in making conversions for common measurements. Or, if you are buying fabric in the U.S.A., use the decimals column and your calculator to figure cost. For example, if you're buying 1⅝ yards of $9.25-a-yard fabric, multiply $9.25 by 1.625 to get a cost of $15.03.

Inches	*Fractions*	*Decimals*	*Meters*
¼"		.25"	.635cm
½"		.5"	1.27cm
¾"		.75"	1.91cm
1"		1.0"	2.54cm
4½"	⅛ yard	.125 yard	11.43cm
9"	¼ yard	.25 yard	22.86c
12"	⅓ yard	.333 yard	.3m
13½"	⅜ yard	.375 yard	.3375m
18"	½ yard	.5 yard	.45m
22½"	⅝ yard	.625 yard	.563m
27"	¾ yard	.75 yard	.675m
31½"	⅞ yard	.875 yard	.788m
36"	1 yard	1 yard	.9m
39⅜"	1¹⁄₁₀ yards	1.1 yards	1m

When you know:	Multiply by:	To find:
inches	25	millimeters (mm)
inches	2.54	centimeters(cm)
inches	0.025	meters (m)
yards	90	centimeters (cm)
yards	0.9	meters (m)

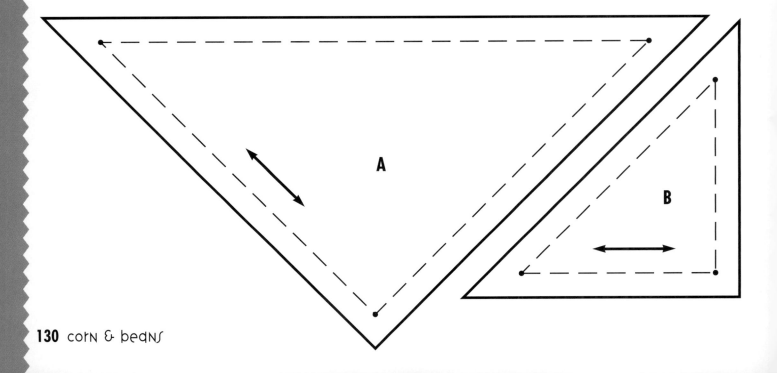

eveNiNg star

Quilt by Darlene C. Christopherson of China Spring, Texas

A beautiful appliquéd border turns this simple wall hanging into a work of art. This is the most basic of appliqué, perfect for a beginner or anyone who loves handwork. The graceful vine surrounds a field of Evening Star blocks. Also known as Sawtooth Star, this block is a patchwork classic, found in some of the earliest existing antique quilts.

Finished Size

Quilt: 41" x 41"
Blocks: 36 blocks, 4" x 4"
This quilt is a wall hanging or crib quilt. Because of the small size of the block, size variations are not recommended for this quilt.

Materials

72 (3" x 9") scraps of blue, rose, and brown prints
1¾ yards background fabric
⅝ yard brown print for inner border and binding
½ yard blue/brown print fabric for vine
⅛ yard blue fabric for sashing squares
1¼ yards backing fabric
44" square batting
½"-wide bias pressing bar

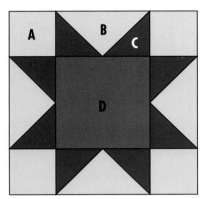

Evening Star Block—Make 36.

Making Blocks

Instructions are for rotary cutting and quick piecing. For appliqué and traditional patchwork techniques, use patterns on page 133.

1. From 36 scrap fabrics, cut one 2½" D square. From each remaining scrap, cut eight 1½" squares for C star points. Save remaining scraps for leaves.
2. From background fabric, cut 14 (1½"-wide) cross-grain strips. From these, cut 144 (1½" x 2½") Bs and 144 (1½") A squares.
3. Referring to page 146, use the diagonal-corner technique to sew two matching C squares to each B rectangle (Diagram A). Or sew C triangles to B traditionally as shown. Make four B/C units for each block. Press seam allowances toward triangles.
4. For each block, select four B/C units, four A squares, and one D square. Sew B/C units to sides of D as shown (Block Assembly Diagram). Press seam allowances toward D. Sew A squares to ends of remaining B/C units; press seam allowances toward squares. Join rows to complete block.
5. Make 36 blocks in this manner.

Quilt Assembly

1. Cut three 4½"-wide cross-grain strips of background fabric. From these, cut 84 (1½" x 4½") sashing strips.
2. From blue fabric, cut 49 (1½") A squares for sashing.
3. For sashing rows, join six sashing strips and seven sashing squares as shown (Row Assembly Diagram). Make seven sashing rows.
4. Lay out blocks in six rows with six blocks in each row, placing sashing between blocks and at row ends. In quilt shown, blocks are placed so that star points of the same color family appear in diagonal rows from top left corner of quilt to bottom right (see photo, page 131). Place sashing rows between block rows.
5. When satisfied with placement of blocks, join blocks in each row.
6. Referring to photo, join blocks rows and sashing rows.

Borders

1. From inner border fabric, cut four 1"-wide cross-grain strips. Set aside the remaining fabric for straight-grain binding and leaves.
2. Referring to page 150, measure quilt from top to bottom and trim two borders to match length. Sew borders to quilt sides.
3. Measure quilt from side to side and trim remaining borders to match quilt width. Sew borders to top and bottom edges of quilt.

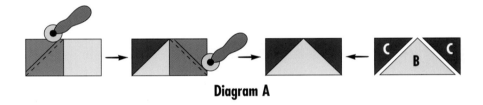

Diagram A

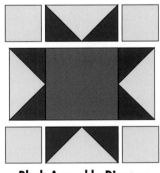

Block Assembly Diagram

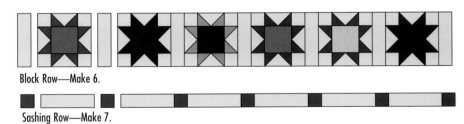

Block Row—Make 6.

Sashing Row—Make 7.

Row Assembly Diagram

4. For outer border, cut four 5"-wide cross-grain strips of background fabric. Referring to pages 150 and 151, sew border strips to quilt and miter corners.

5. Referring to page 156, make 178" of 1½"-wide continuous bias. See PinPoints on page 134 for tips on preparing bias for appliqué.

6. Use a pin to mark the center of each outer border strip, 1½" from bottom edge. To mark high and low placement points for vine, measure 4½"-wide border segments on both sides of the center point, marking each spot with a pin 1" below the inner border seam or 1½" from bottom edge **(Diagram B)**. Place seven pins on each border. At each corner, measure 3½" from last pin to mark outer edge of corner curve.

7. Starting at any side, baste prepared bias strip onto outer border. Curve bias up and down, matching pin placement points and removing pins as you go **(Diagram B)**. Curve bias around corners with bottom of curve at mitered seam. When satisfied with position of bias, trim excess and overlap ends as necessary. Appliqué bias vine in place.

8. From remaining scrap fabrics, cut 260 leaves. Prepare leaves for appliqué.

9. Referring to photo, pin about 65 leaves on each border, overlapping vine as desired. Cover ends of bias with one or more leaves to hide overlap. When satisfied with placement, appliqué leaves in place.

Quilting and Finishing

1. Mark quilting design on quilt top as desired. Quilt shown has diagonal lines quilted over the quilt surface, spaced ¼" apart.

2. Layer backing, batting, and quilt top. Backing seams run parallel to top and bottom edges of quilt. Baste. Quilt as desired.

3. Make 4¾ yards of straight-grain binding. See page 156 for instructions on making and applying binding.

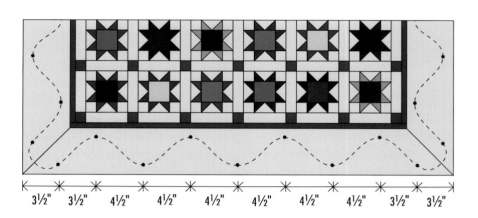

3½" 3½" 4½" 4½" 4½" 4½" 4½" 4½" 3½" 3½"

Diagram B

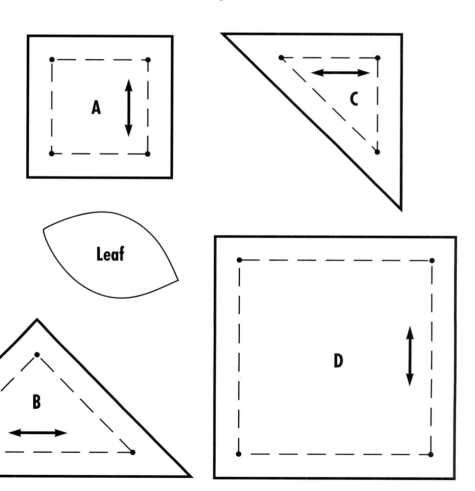

Bias Appliqué

Make curvy appliquéd vines and flower stems from bias strips. Use *bias pressing bars* of metal or heat-resistant plastic to prepare bias for appliqué. Available in various widths, bias bars are sold at quilt shops and through mail-order catalogs.

1. Start with a square of fabric. Instructions state the size of the square and the width of the strips to be cut. Cut the square in half diagonally to get two triangles. See page 156 for instructions on making continuous bias. Or cut bias strips, measuring from the cut edge of each triangle **(Photo A)**.

2. Fold strip in half lengthwise, with wrong sides facing and long edges together. Stitch ¼" from the edges, making a narrow tube. Slide the tube over the pressing bar, centering the seam on the flat side of the bar **(Photo B)**.

3. Press seam allowance to one side or open, as you like **(Photo C)**. Be careful when handling metal bars—they get hot! Remove the bar when pressing is complete. Trim seam allowance if needed.

4. With the seam against the background fabric, baste or pin the bias strip in place **(Photo D)**. A steam iron will help shape the strip. Appliqué the strip onto the background fabric, sewing inside curves first and then the outside curves so that the bias will lie flat.

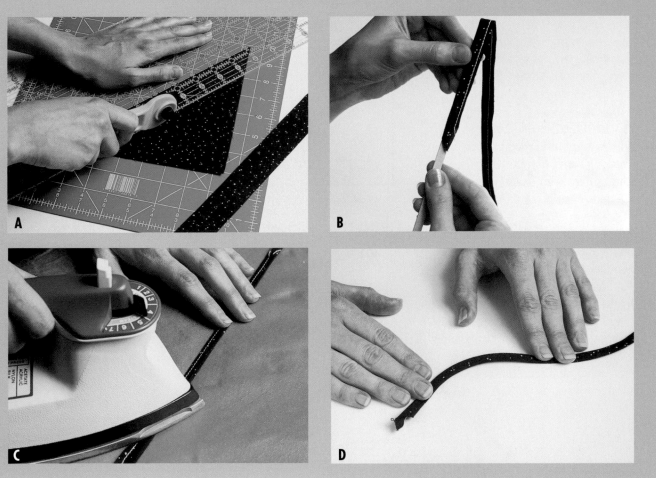

flock of geese

Once in a blue moon, you might host a sewing bee. Pick a color theme and invite friends to bring scraps in that color. You can't go wrong with blue because, no matter what color is a quilter's favorite, everybody has lots of blue! Quick-pieced triangle-squares are easy to sew and fun to make—they're ideal for swapping with friends. Spend an afternoon sharing good cheer as well as cutting and sewing, and everyone will go home with enough blocks for a quilt.

Finished Size

Quilt: 61" x 81"
Blocks: 35 blocks, 10" x 10"
This quilt fits a twin-size bed.
See Size Variations (page 138)
for other size requirements.

Materials

35 (8" x 14") blue scraps
35 (8" x 14") white scraps
¾ yard inner border fabric*
2¼ yards outer border fabric
⅞ yard binding fabric
4 yards backing fabric
72" x 90" precut batting

*Note: Yardage is for pieced borders. If you prefer not to piece borders, you need 2¼ yards to cut lengthwise strips.

Quilt by Lenel W. Walsh of Austin, Texas

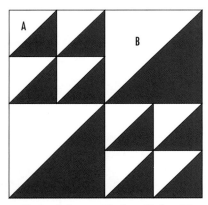

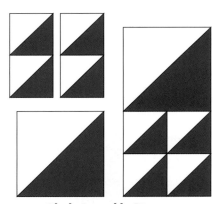

Flock of Geese Block—Make 35.

Block Assembly Diagram

Making Blocks

Instructions are for rotary cutting and quick piecing. See page 149 for directions on quick-pieced triangle-squares. For traditional cutting and piecing, use patterns A and B on page 138.

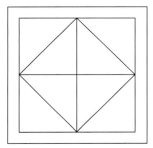

Diagram A

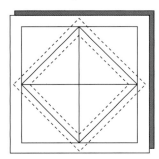

Diagram B

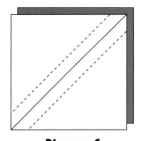

Diagram C

1. Select one blue fabric and one white fabric for each block. From each fabric, cut one 8" square for A triangle-squares and one 5⅞" square for B triangle-squares.
2. On wrong side of 8" white square, mark a 2-square x 2-square grid of 3⅜" squares as shown (**Diagram A**). Mark diagonal lines through centers of squares as shown.
3. Match white and blue squares, right sides facing. Stitch on both sides of diagonal lines as shown (**Diagram B**). Press stitching.
4. Cut on drawn lines to get eight A triangle-squares. Press seam allowances toward dark fabric.
5. On wrong side of remaining white square, draw a diagonal line from corner to corner. Match white and blue squares, right sides facing. Stitch on both sides of diagonal line as shown (**Diagram C**). Press. Cut on drawn line to get two B triangle-squares. Press seam allowances toward dark fabric.

6. Join A triangle-squares to make four pairs (**Block Assembly Diagram**). Then join pairs to make two four-patch units as shown. Be sure to position all triangles in the same direction as shown. Press.
7. Join a B triangle-square to one side of each four-patch, positioning triangle-squares as shown to make two half-blocks. Press joining seam allowances toward B triangle-squares. Join halves to complete block.
8. In this manner, make 35 blocks.

Quilt Assembly

1. For each horizontal row, lay out five blocks as shown (**Row Assembly Diagram**). Lay out seven rows. Rearrange blocks as desired to achieve a pleasing balance of fabrics. When satisfied with placement, join blocks in each row.
2. Referring to photo, join rows.

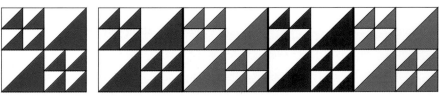

Row Assembly Diagram

Borders

1. From inner border fabric, cut eight 2½"-wide crosswise strips. Join two strips end-to-end to make each border.
2. Referring to page 150, measure quilt from top to bottom and trim side borders to match length. Sew borders to quilt sides.
3. Measure quilt from side to side and trim remaining borders to match quilt width. Sew borders to top and bottom edges of quilt.
4. From outer border fabric, cut four 4"-wide lengthwise border strips. Measure quilt, trim, and sew outer borders as for inner border.

Quilting and Finishing

1. Mark quilting design on quilt top as desired. Quilt shown has an allover pattern of machine quilting.
2. Divide backing into two equal lengths. Cut one piece in half lengthwise. Join a narrow panel to each side of wide piece to assemble backing.
3. Layer backing, batting, and quilt top. Backing seams will be parallel to top and bottom edges of quilt. Baste. Quilt as desired.
4. Make 8¼ yards of bias or straight-grain binding. See page 156 for instructions on making and applying binding.

Birds of a Different Color

If blue just isn't you, make birds of a different feather. To stir your imagination, we've illustrated a few alternatives—just imagine exotic green parrots, sassy red cardinals, or an aviary of pastel canaries, love birds, and parakeets.

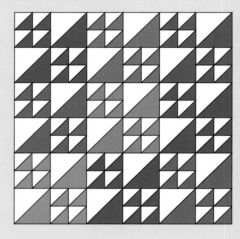

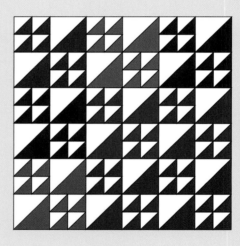

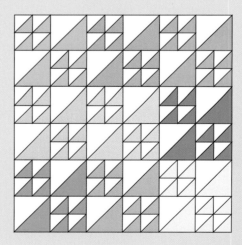

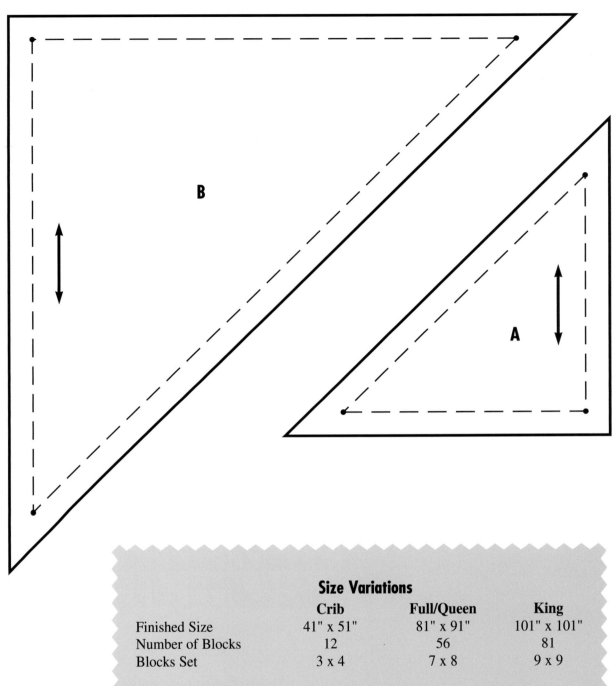

Size Variations

	Crib	Full/Queen	King
Finished Size	41" x 51"	81" x 91"	101" x 101"
Number of Blocks	12	56	81
Blocks Set	3 x 4	7 x 8	9 x 9
Yardage Required			
Blue scraps	12	56	81
White scraps	12	56	81
Inner border fabric	⅜ yard	¾ yard	1 yard
Outer border fabric	1½ yards	2¾ yards	3 yards
Backing fabric	1½ yards	5¾ yards	6 yards
Binding fabric	½ yard	1 yard	1 yard

step-by-step guide to Quiltmaking

Fabric Preparation

Lightweight, 100%-cotton fabric is the best choice for quilts. Sturdy and durable, cotton is neither stretchy nor tightly woven and it takes a crease well, so seams are easy to press. When you use good quality fabric, your quilt looks nice and lasts a long time.

Selecting Fabric

Choosing fabric seems to bring out insecurities in many quiltmakers. Will my quilt look as good as the one in the picture? If I change the color to blue, will my quilt look as nice as the green one?

Trust Your Instincts. There are no right or wrong choices, nor are there any hard-and-fast rules governing fabric selection. Go with fabrics you like. You can ask for help from family and friends, but the final choice should be yours.

Work with the staff at your local quilt shop. Take down half the bolts in the store, if necessary, to try different combinations. Group your choices on a table and then—this is very important—step back at least 8 feet and squint. This gives you a preview of the mix of value and texture. If a fabric looks out of place, replace it and try again. And again. And again, until you're satisfied.

Prewashing

Wash, dry, and iron all fabrics before cutting to eliminate the center crease, as well as excess dye and sizing. Also, fabric can shrink slightly after washing. If you take the time to prewash, there's less chance of damage occurring later.

Use the washer and detergent that you'll use to wash the finished quilt.

Wash light and dark colors separately in warm water. Use a mild detergent or Orvus Paste, a mild soap available at many quilt shops.

Test for Colorfastness. Today's improved dyes and processes mean that bleeding is not the problem that it was in your grandmother's time. Nonetheless, you want to be sure to remove excess dye before you use any fabric. If you don't, you risk the fabric bleeding onto another when the finished quilt is washed.

After machine washing the fabric, rinse each piece in the sink, adding a clean scrap of white fabric. If the scrap becomes stained, rinse again with a clean scrap. Continue until the scrap remains white.

If repeated rinsing doesn't stop the bleeding, don't use that fabric—take it back to the store where you bought it and *complain!*

Dry and Press. Dry prewashed fabrics in the dryer at a medium or permanent-press setting until they're just damp. Then press them dry. It's important to iron out all creases and folds so you'll have smooth, straight fabric with which to work.

Grain Lines

The interwoven lengthwise and crosswise threads of a fabric are grain lines. Think about grain direction before you cut. Cotton fabric can be stable or stretchy, depending on how it is cut.

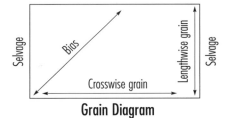

Grain Diagram

Selvage. The lengthwise finished edges of the uncut fabric are selvages (**Grain Diagram**). These edges are more tightly woven than the body of the fabric and are sometimes not printed. Always trim selvage from the ends of a strip before cutting pieces for your quilt.

Straight Grain. Lengthwise grain, parallel to the selvage, has the least give. Long strips for sashing and borders, which must retain their shape over time, are best cut lengthwise for stability.

Crosswise grain, perpendicular to the selvage, has more give. For most patchwork pieces, strips are cut on the crosswise grain but either direction is acceptable.

Bias. True bias is at a 45° angle to the selvages, on the diagonal between lengthwise and crosswise grains (**Grain Diagram**). Bias-cut fabric has the most stretch. When you cut a triangle, at least one edge is bias. Handle a bias edge carefully, as it can easily stretch out of shape, warping the patchwork.

Bedcover Size Variations

We give instructions for each quilt in one size, and, when possible, we give bonus sizing information. Even so, you might want to make adjustments to suit a quilt intended for a particular bed. Consider the quilt's design, the bed's size and style, and your own preferences.

Lap quilts, doll quilts, wall hangings, or quilts "just for show" can be any size you like.

Get a Good Fit

The bed style will influence a quilt's finished size. For example, a quilt for a four-poster needs more length and width than one made for a contemporary platform-style bed.

On most beds, a quilt's length and width is affected by whether you use a dust ruffle or let the quilt hang past the box spring, or even to the floor. Also consider the bed's height and whether you want a pillow tuck or to let the quilt lie flat.

Standard Sizes

Once you choose the look you want, refer to the chart below to find the mattress size and the dimensions of the corresponding style of bedcover.

Comforters. Most comforters cover the mattress but not the box spring, nor do they allow for pillow tuck. Treat comforter dimensions as minimum standards if you want to use your quilt with a dust ruffle and decorative pillows.

Bedspreads. A bedspread covers the bed, falls almost to the floor, and allows for a pillow tuck. These sizes are maximum proportions, assuming the top of the mattress is a standard 20" from the floor.

Custom Calculations. The information below gives average dimensions for four popular bed sizes. These dimensions include a 12" drop on three sides and 8" for a pillow tuck. But if your needs differ, here's how to calculate the best finished size for your quilt.

Start with the mattress dimensions. If you want a pillow tuck, add 8"–10" to the length.

To determine the length of the drop, measure from the top of the mattress to just below the top of the dust ruffle, all the way to the floor, or some desired point in between. For most quilts, you'll add one drop to the length and two drops to the width.

Example. Let's figure the size of a quilt for a queen-size bed. For this example, we'll assume a 12" drop is wanted, but no extra is needed for a pillow tuck.

We know the mattress measures 60" x 80". To figure the quilt width, add 12" twice to the width of the mattress: 60" + 12" + 12" = 84". To figure the quilt's length, add 12" to the length of the mattress: 80" + 12" = 92".

Finally, remember that the finished size you determine (and the size given with instructions) is a mathematical calculation—the finished size will vary slightly with the effects of sewing and quilting.

Adapting a Design to Fit

If the quilt you plan to make is not the size you want, there are several ways to adapt the design.

To make a smaller quilt, eliminate a row of blocks, set the blocks without sashing, and/or narrow the border widths.

To make a quilt larger, add rows of blocks, sashing, and/or multiple borders. Each addition requires extra yardage, which you should estimate before you buy fabric.

	Standard Mattress Size*	Comforter Size	Bedspread Size	Our Average Quilt Size**
Twin	38" x 75"	58" x 86"	80" x 108"	62" x 95"
Full	53" x 75"	73" x 86"	96" x 108"	77" x 95"
Queen	60" x 80"	80" x 88"	102" x 118"	84" x 100"
King	76" x 80"	96" x 88"	120" x 118"	100" x 100"

*Standards for spring mattresses; waterbeds may vary.
**Includes 12" drop at end and sides, as well as 8" for pillow tuck.

Rotary Cutting

Rotary cutting is fast and easy. It's fast because you measure and cut with one stroke, skipping steps of making templates and marking fabric. It's accurate because the fabric stays flat as you cut, instead of being raised by a scissor blade. If rotary cutting is new to you, use these instructions to practice on scraps. Rotary cutting may seem strange at first, but give it a try—you'll love it!

Rotary cutting often begins with cutting fabric strips which are then cut into smaller pieces. Unless specified otherwise, cut strips crosswise, selvage to selvage.

Instructions specify the number and width of strips needed, as well as the size and quantity of pieces to cut from these strips. *Seam allowances are included in measurements given for all strips and pieces.*

A rotary cutter is fun to use, but it is very sharp and should be handled with caution. Carelessness can result in cutting yourself, other people, or objects that you had no intention of slicing. Always keep the safety guard in place on the cutter until you're ready to use it. In use or in storage, keep the cutter out of reach of children.

---

1 Cutters, mats, and rulers come in many sizes and styles. Choose a cutter that is comfortable to hold. Change the blade when it becomes dull. The most useful cutting mat is 24" x 36", but you may want a smaller one for cutting scraps.

Rotary-cutting rulers are made of thick, transparent acrylic. Select rulers that are marked in increments of 1", ¼", and ⅛". A 45°-angle line is also useful. Rulers are available in many sizes and shapes. The most popular rulers are a 6" x 24" for cutting long strips, a 15" square, and a 6" x 12" for small cuts.

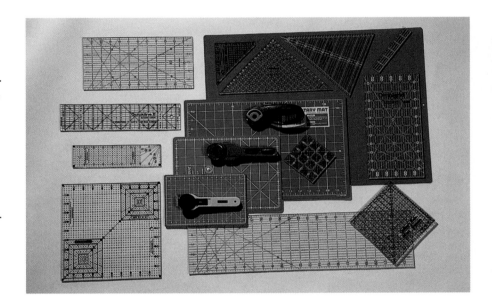

2 To cut straight strips, you must square up an edge. Start by folding the fabric in half, matching selvages. Fold again, aligning the selvage with the first fold to make four layers. Let the yardage extend to the right, leaving the end to be cut on the mat. (Reverse directions if you are left-handed.)

3 Align the edge of a large square ruler with the bottom fold. The left edge of the square should be about 1" from the rough edge of the fabric. Butt a long ruler against the left side of the square, overlapping top and bottom fabric edges. Remove the square, keeping the long ruler in place.

4 **Holding the long ruler** still with your left hand, place the cutter blade against the ruler at the bottom of the mat. Begin rolling the cutter before it meets the fabric, moving it away from you. Use firm, even pressure, keeping the ruler stable and the blade against the ruler. Do not lift the cutter until it cuts through the opposite edge of the fabric.

5 **To measure the strip width,** place the ruler on the left edge of the fabric. Carefully align the desired measurement on the ruler with the fabric, checking the ruler line from top to bottom of the fabric. Cut, holding the ruler firmly in place. A sharp blade cuts easily through four layers.

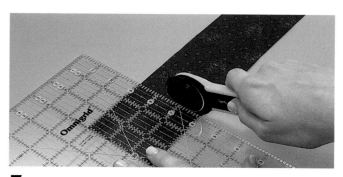

6 **Check the cut strip.** If the fabric edge is not squared up properly, the strip will bow in the middle (top, above). If necessary, square up the edge again and cut another strip. When satisfied with cut strips, rotary-cut ½" from the strip ends to remove selvages.

7 **To cut squares and rectangles** from a strip, align the desired measurement on the ruler with the end of the strip. Check the ruler alignment from top to bottom as well as side to side to be sure the ruler is straight. When satisfied with ruler alignment, cut.

8 **For right triangles,** instructions may say to cut a square in half or in quarters diagonally. This works with rectangles, too. The edges of the square or rectangle are straight grain, so the triangle's diagonal edges, from the inside of the square, are bias. Handle these edges with care to keep the fabric from stretching as you work with it.

9 **Keep cut pieces** and sewn units neatly stored. If you constantly move your work on and off the dining room table, it's easy to get pieces mixed up. Store cut pieces in zip-top plastic bags labeled with the appropriate unit number. If the sewing takes several weeks, your pieces won't get lost, mixed up, or dirty. Remove one piece at a time as you work.

Cutting with Templates

A template is a duplication of a printed pattern that you use to trace a shape onto fabric. Use templates to accurately mark curves and complex shapes. For straight-sided shapes, it is a matter of preference whether you use templates or a rotary cutter and ruler.

Oxmoor House patterns are full-size. Patterns for pieced blocks show the seam line (dashed) and the cutting line (solid). Appliqué patterns do not include seam allowances. To make a template from dimensions given for rotary cutting, use a ruler to draw a pattern onto template material.

We recommend template plastic, which is easy to cut and can be used repeatedly without fraying or cracking. Best of all, the transparency of the plastic allows you to trace a pattern directly onto it. Templates made of this plastic are more reliable than those cut from cardboard or sandpaper.

To check the accuracy of your templates, cut and piece a test block before cutting more pieces.

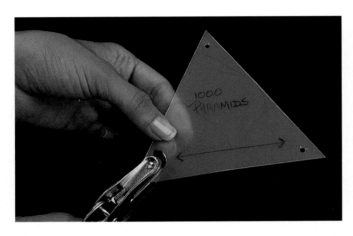

1 Trace the pattern onto plastic, using a ruler to draw straight lines. If desired, punch ⅛"-diameter holes at the corners of the template's seam line to enable you to mark pivot points.

2 For piecing, trace around the template on the wrong side of the fabric. For symmetrical pieces like squares and some right triangles, it doesn't matter whether the template is faceup or facedown. But if the template is not symmetrical, always place it facedown on the wrong side of the fabric. Use common lines for efficient cutting.

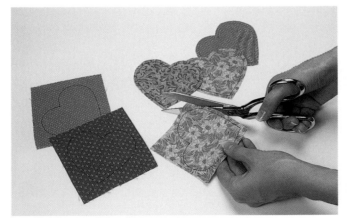

3 For appliqué, trace template on right side of fabric. (A lightly drawn line disappears into the fold of the seam allowance when the piece is stitched to the background fabric.) Position tracings at least ½" apart so you can add seam allowances when cutting each piece.

4 A window template provides the guidance of a drawn seam line, which is very useful for sewing a set-in seam. When traced on the right side of the fabric, a window template can help you to center specific motifs with accuracy.

Machine-Piecing Basics

A consistent ¼" seam allowance is essential for accurate piecing. If each seam varies by the tiniest bit, the difference multiplies greatly by the time a block is complete. Be sure your machine is in good order and that you can sew a precise ¼" seam allowance.

On some sewing machines, you can position the needle to sew a ¼" seam. Or use a presser foot that measures ¼" from the needle to the outside edge of the foot. These feet are available at sewing supply stores. If neither option is available, make a seam guide as described under Photo 1.

To test your seam allowance, cut three 1½" fabric squares and join them in a row. Press the seams and measure the strip. If it's not precisely 3½" long, try again with a deeper or shallower seam allowance.

Set your sewing machine to 12–14 stitches per inch. Use 100% cotton or cotton/polyester sewing thread.

With right sides facing, sew each seam from cut edge to cut edge of the fabric. It is not necessary to backstitch, because most seams are crossed and held by another.

The following are other points that will make machine piecing easy.

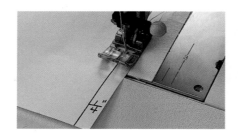

1 Use a ruler and a sharp pencil to draw a line ¼" from the edge of a piece of paper. Lower the machine needle onto the line, drop the foot, and adjust the paper to parallel the foot. Lay masking tape on the throat plate at the edge of the paper. Sew a seam to test the guide. If seam allowances get wider or narrower, the tape is not straight.

3 To press, use an up-and-down motion. (Sliding the iron can push seams out of shape.) Press the seam flat on the wrong side. Then open the fabric to the right side and press seam allowances to one side, not open as in dressmaking. Press seam allowances in opposite directions so they offset where seams meet. If possible, press seam allowances toward a dark fabric.

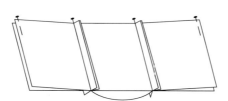

5 Sometimes two units that should match are slightly different. To join these units, pin-match seams and sew with the shorter piece on top. The feed dogs ease the fullness on the bottom piece. If units are too different to ease, resew the one that varies most from the desired size.

2 When you piece triangles with other units, seams should cross in an X on the back. When these units are joined, the joining seam should go precisely through the center of the X so the triangle will have a nice sharp point on the front.

4 Use pins to match seam lines. With right sides facing, align opposing seams, nesting seam allowances. On the top piece, push a pin through the seam line ¼" from the edge. Then push the pin through the bottom seam and set it. Pin all matching seams; then stitch the joining seam, removing pins as you sew.

6 Chain piecing is an efficient way to sew many units in one operation, saving time and thread. Sew one unit as usual, but at the end of the seam do not clip the thread or lift the presser foot. Instead, feed in the next unit on the heels of the first, assembly-line style. Sew as many seams as you like on a chain. Clip the threads as you press.

Quick-Piecing Techniques

The methods explained here are uniquely suited to machine sewing. Combined with rotary cutting, they reduce cutting and sewing time without sacrificing results. Before starting your quilt, practice a required technique that is new to you. You'll love how fast and easy the pieces come together!

Diagonal Corners turn squares into sewn triangles with just a stitch and a snip. This technique is particularly helpful if the corner triangle is very small, because it's easier to cut and handle a square than a small triangle. By sewing squares to squares, you don't have to guess where seam allowances meet, which can be difficult with triangles.

Project instructions give the size of the fabric pieces needed. The base fabric is either a square or a rectangle, but the contrasting corner always starts out as a square.

Diagonal Ends are sewn in a similar manner as diagonal corners. This method joins two rectangles on the diagonal without your having to measure and cut a trapezoid. Project instructions specify the size of each rectangle. To sew diagonal ends, make a seam guide for your sewing machine as described in Step 1 for diagonal corners.

Strip Piecing requires you to join strips of different fabrics to make a strip set. From these, you cut segments that become units of patchwork. Project directions specify how to cut strips and each strip set is illustrated. This is a fast and accurate technique because you sew and press the strip set *before* you cut individual units.

Diagonal Corners

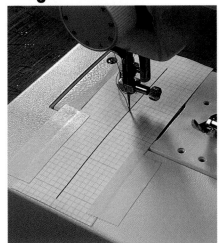

1 Make a seam guide that will help you sew diagonal lines without having to mark the fabric beforehand. Draw a line on paper. Lower the needle onto the line. (Remove the foot if necessary for a good viewpoint.) Use a ruler to confirm that the line is parallel to the needle. Tape the paper in place; then trim it as needed to clear the needle and feed dogs.

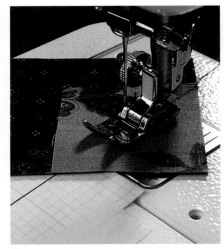

2 Match the small square to one corner of the base fabric, right sides facing. Align the top tip of the small square with the needle and the bottom tip with the seam guide. Stitch a diagonal seam from tip to tip, keeping the bottom tip of the small square in line with the seam guide.

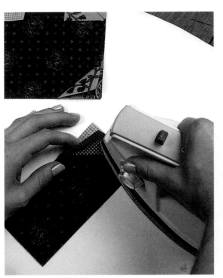

3 Press the small square in half at the seam.

4 Trim the seam allowance to ¼". Repeat the procedure as needed to add a diagonal corner to two, three, or four corners of the base fabric. This technique is the same when you add a diagonal corner to a strip set or a diagonal end—treat the base fabric as one piece, even if it is already pieced.

Diagonal Ends

1 **Position rectangles** perpendicular to each other with right sides facing, matching corners to be sewn. Before you sew, pin on the stitching line and check the right side to see if the line is angled in the desired direction.

Position the rectangles under the needle, leading with the top edge. Sew a diagonal seam to the opposite edge.

2 **Check the right side** to see that the seam is angled correctly. Then press the seam and trim excess fabric from the seam allowance.

As noted in Step 1, the direction of the seam makes a difference. Make mirror-image units with this in mind, or you can put different ends on the same strip.

Strip Piecing

1 **To sew a strip set,** match each pair of strips with right sides facing. Sew through both layers along one long edge. As you add strips to the set, sew each new seam in the opposite direction from the last one. This distributes tension evenly in both directions and keeps the strip set from getting warped and wobbly.

2 **When a strip set** is assembled and pressed, you will be directed to cut it into segments. Use a ruler to measure; then make appropriate crosswise cuts to get individual segments.

Quick-Pieced Triangle-Squares

Many patchwork designs are made by joining contrasting triangles to make triangle-squares. These can consist of two or four contrasting right triangles.

Cutting and sewing triangles pose unique problems for quilters. These quick-piecing techniques eliminate those difficulties and enable you to create many pre-sewn units with one process—a real time-saver.

These instructions use a grid method. A grid is marked on the fabric and then stitched as described below.

Cutting instructions specify two fabric rectangles for each grid. We recommend that you spray both pieces with spray starch to keep the fabric from distorting during marking and stitching. For marking, use a see-through ruler and a fine-tipped fabric pen—a pencil drags on the fabric, making an inaccurate line and stretching the fabric. Accuracy is important in every step—if your marking, cutting, sewing, and pressing are not precise, your triangle-squares may be lopsided or the wrong size.

Two-Triangle Squares

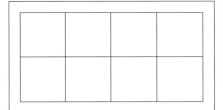

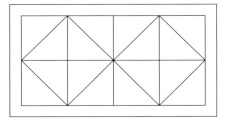

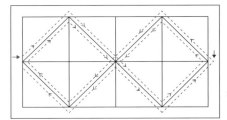

1 **For our example,** let's say instructions call for a 2 x 4 grid of 2⅞" squares. This describes a grid of eight squares, drawn two down and four across. Draw the grid on the wrong side of the lighter fabric. The fabric size specified allows a margin of at least 1" around the grid, so align the ruler parallel to one long edge of the fabric, 1" from the edge, and draw the first line.

Draw the second line exactly 2⅞" below the first. Continue in this manner, using the ruler's markings to position each new line. Take care to make lines accurately parallel and/or perpendicular.

2 **When the grid** is completely drawn, draw a diagonal line through each square. Alternate direction of diagonals in adjacent squares.

In this example, we're working toward a desired finished size of 2" square. The grid squares are drawn ⅞" larger than the finished size. After the grid is sewn, the cut and pressed square is ½" larger than the finished size (2½").

3 **With right sides facing,** match edges of the two fabric pieces. Start near the left corner of the grid (blue arrow). Sewing a ¼" seam allowance, stitch alongside the diagonals indicated by the blue line. At the end of one line, stitch into the margin as shown. Keep the needle down, raise the foot, and pivot the fabric to stitch the next line. When you return to the start, you'll have sewn one side of all diagonal lines.

Begin again at another point (red arrow). Repeat stitching on the opposite side of the diagonal lines. When the grid is completely stitched, press the fabric to smooth the stitching.

4 **Rotary-cut on** all the drawn lines to separate the triangle-squares. Each grid square yields two triangle-squares, so our example will produce 16 units.

5 **Press each triangle-square** open, pressing the seam allowance toward the darker fabric. Trim points from ends of each seam allowance.

Traditional Appliqué

Appliqué is the process of sewing pieces onto a background to create a fabric picture. The edges of appliqué pieces are turned under and sewn to the background by hand or machine.

For hand appliqué, the edges of each piece must be turned under by hand. You can avoid this with some machine techniques. Usually, however, machine appliqué is accomplished by preparing pieces in the same manner and using a topstitch or blindhem stitch to secure them to the background.

For traditional hand appliqué, follow steps 1–2 at right. See page 144, Step 3, for tips on making templates and cutting appliqué pieces. Some quilters find it easier to turn edges with freezer-paper templates as described below.

1 **For traditional hand appliqué,** use the drawn line as a guide to turn under seam allowances on each piece. Do not turn an edge that will be covered by another piece. Hand-baste seam allowances. (You can eliminate basting, if you prefer, and rely on rolling the edge under with the tip of your needle as you sew. This is called needle-turned appliqué.) Pin appliqué pieces to the background fabric.

2 **Slipstitch** around each piece, using thread that matches the appliqué. (We used contrasting thread for photography.) Pull the needle through the background and catch a few threads on the fold of the appliqué. Reinsert the needle into the background and bring the needle up through the appliqué for the next stitch. Make close, tiny stitches that do not show on the right side. Remove basting.

Freezer Paper Appliqué

Usually, you'll trace a full-size pattern onto the dull side of freezer paper. When working with freezer paper, the finished appliqué is a mirror image of the pattern. So, if the pattern is an irregular shape (not symmetrical), first make a tracing paper pattern so you can turn it over when you trace the shape onto freezer paper and prevent the appliqué from being reversed. Cut out paper templates on the drawn lines.

Use a dry iron at wool setting to press shiny side of paper template to wrong side of fabric. Allow at least ½" between templates for seam allowances.

1 **Cut out appliqué pieces,** adding ¼" seam allowance around each shape. With small, sharp scissors, snip seam allowance at curves, clipping halfway to paper edge. This allows the seam allowance to spread when turned so curve will lie flat.

2 **Apply fabric glue** to the wrong side of each seam allowance. Use your fingers or a cool, dry iron to turn the seam allowances over the edges of the template where the glue will secure them to the paper. Do not turn edges that will be covered by another appliqué piece. Pin and sew pieces in place as described in steps 1 and 2 above.

3 **When stitching** is complete, turn the work to the wrong side. Cut background fabric from behind the appliqué, leaving scant ¼" seam allowances. Moisten the fabric with a spray of water to dissolve the glue. Use tweezers to remove the paper pieces.

Joining Blocks

The easiest way to join blocks is in rows, either vertically, horizontally, or diagonally.

Arrange blocks and setting pieces, if any, on the floor or a large table. Identify the pieces in each row and verify the position of each block. This is playtime—moving the blocks around to find the best balance of color and value is great fun. Don't start sewing until you're happy with the placement of each block.

As you join blocks in each row, pick up one block at a time to avoid confusion. Pin-match adjoining seams. Re-press a seam if necessary to offset seam allowances. If you find some blocks are larger than others, pinning may help determine where easing is required. A blast of steam from the iron may help fit the blocks together.

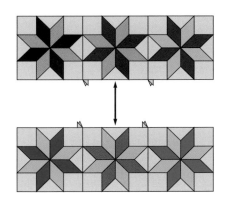

1 **Press seam allowances** between blocks in the same direction. From row to row, press in opposite directions so that seam allowances will offset when rows are joined.

3 **Sashing eliminates** questions about pressing. Just remember to always press toward the sashing. Assemble rows with sashing strips between blocks, and press the new seam allowances toward the sashing. If necessary, ease the block to match the length of the strip. Assemble the quilt with rows of sashing between block rows.

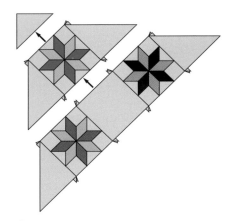

2 **In an alternate set,** straight or diagonal, press seam allowances between blocks toward setting squares or triangles. This creates the least bulk and always results in opposing seam allowances when adjacent rows are joined.

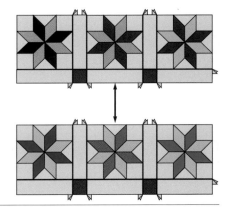

Borders

Most quilts have one or more borders that frame the central design. Borders can be plain, pieced, or appliquéd; corners are square or mitered.

The colors, shapes, and proportions of border pieces should complement those in the quilt. The color of an outside border makes that color dominant in the quilt. For example, if a quilt has equal amounts of red, white, and blue, a blue border emphasizes blue in the pieced design.

Measuring

It's common for one side of a sewn quilt to be a slightly different measurement than its opposite side. Little variables in cutting and piecing add up. Sew borders of equal length to opposite sides to square up the quilt.

Most cutting instructions include extra length for border strips to allow for piecing variations. Before sewing them, trim border strips to fit your quilt properly. How you measure, trim, and sew border strips depends on the type of corner you're making.

Square Corners. Measure from top to bottom through the middle of the quilt, edge to edge (**Diagram 1**). Trim side borders to this length and sew them to the quilt sides. You may

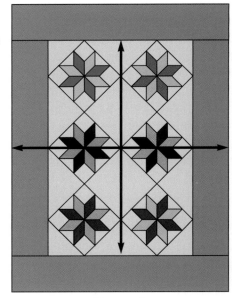

Diagram 1

need to ease one side of a quilt to fit the border and then stretch the opposite side to fit the same border length. In the end, both sides will be the same.

For top and bottom borders, measure from side to side through the middle of the quilt, including side borders and seam allowances. Trim remaining borders to this length and sew them to the quilt.

Mitered Corners. The seam of a mitered corner is more subtle than that of a square corner, so it creates the illusion of a continuous line around the quilt. Mitered corners are particularly suitable for borders of striped fabric, pieced borders, or multiple plain borders. Multiple borders should be sewn together and the resulting striped units treated as a single border for mitering.

First, measure the quilt's length through the middle **(Diagram 2)**. Subtract ½" for seam allowances at the outer edges. Mark the center of each border strip. Working out from the center, measure and mark the determined length on the border strip.

Measure the quilt's width and repeat marking on remaining border strips. Do not trim borders until after corner seam is sewn.

Diagram 2

Sewing a Mitered Corner

1 **On the wrong side** of each edge of the quilt, mark the center and each corner, ¼" from the edge. These marks correspond to marks on each border strip. Pin borders to quilt with right sides together, matching marked points.

2 **Backstitching** at both ends, sew the border seam from match point to match point, easing as needed. Join remaining borders in the same manner. (We've used contrasting thread for photography.)

3 **Fold the quilt** at one corner to align adjacent borders, right sides together. Align ruler with the fold of the quilt. Along the edge of the ruler (which is at a 45° angle to the border), draw a line from the corner of the seam to the outside edge. This is the sewing line for the miter.

 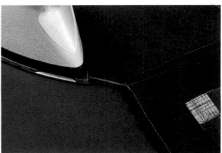

4 **Beginning with a backstitch** at the inside corner, stitch on the marked line to the outside edge. Check the right side to see that the seam lies flat and stripes match. When satisfied with mitered seam, trim excess fabric to a ¼" seam allowance.

5 **Press mitered seam open** or to one side, as you prefer, so that the interior portion of the quilt lies flat. Then press the seam on the right side of the quilt.

Marking a Quilting Design

The quilting design is an important part of any quilt, so choose it with care. The hours you spend stitching together the layers of your quilt create shadows and depths that bring the quilt to life, so make the design count.

Most quilters mark a quilting design on the quilt top before it is layered and basted. To do this, you need marking pencils, a long ruler or yardstick, stencils for quilting motifs, and a smooth, hard surface on which to work. Press the quilt top thoroughly before you begin.

To find a stencil for a quilting design, check your local quilt shop or mail-order catalogs for one that suits your quilt. Or, if you know what kind of design you want, make your own stencil.

Test Markers

Before using any marker, test it on scraps to be sure marks will wash out. Don't use just any pencil because that's what your grandmother used. There are many pencils and chalk markers available that are designed to wash out. No matter what marking tool you use, lightly drawn lines are easier to remove than heavy ones.

Marking a Grid

Many quilts feature a grid of squares or diamonds as a quilting design in the background areas of the quilt. Use a ruler to mark a grid, starting at one border seam and working toward the opposite edge. Mark parallel lines, spacing them as desired (usually 1" apart), until background areas are marked as desired.

Stencils

1 **To transfer a design** to the quilt top, position the stencil on the quilt and mark through the slits in the stencil. Connect the lines after removing the stencil.

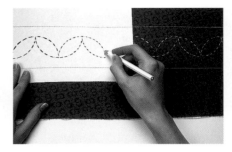

2 **To make a stencil,** trace a design onto freezer paper or template plastic. Use a craft knife to cut little slots along the lines of the design. Place the stencil on the fabric and mark in each slot.

Quilting Without Marking

Some quilts are quilted in-the-ditch (right in the seams) or outline-quilted (¼" from the seam line). These methods do not require marking.

If you are machine quilting, use the edge of your presser foot and the seam line as guides for outline quilting. If you are hand quilting, use narrow drafting tape as a guideline between the seam and the quilting line.

Another option is stippling—freestyle, meandering lines of quilting worked closely together to fill open areas. This can be done by hand or by machine, letting your needle go where the mood takes you.

Making a Backing

The backing should be at least 3" larger than the quilt top on all sides. For quilts up to 40" wide, use one length of 45"-wide cotton fabric. For a large quilt, 90"- or 108"-wide fabric is a sensible option that reduces waste. But selection is limited in wide fabrics, so many quilters piece two or three lengths of 45"-wide fabric to make a backing.

Choose a light backing fabric for light-colored quilts, because you don't want a dark color to show through. To show off your stitching, select a plain fabric. If you don't want to showcase your quilting this way, choose a busy print for the backing as camouflage or piece the backing from assorted scraps.

Most quilt backs have two or three seams **(Backing Options Diagram)** to avoid having a seam in the center back. (Many experts feel that a center seam augments the creases formed by routine folding of a quilt.) Press seam allowances open.

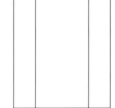 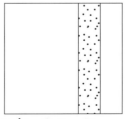 

Backing Options Diagram

Batting

When selecting batting, consider loft, washability, and fiber content. Read the package label to decide if a particular product suits your needs.

Precut batting comes in five sizes. The precut batt listed for each quilt is the most suitable for the quilt's finished size. Some stores sell 90"-wide batting by the yard, which might be more practical for your quilt.

Loft. Loft is the height or thickness of the batting. For a traditional flat look, choose low-loft cotton batting. Polyester batting is available in medium and low lofts that are suitable for most quilts. Thick batting is difficult to quilt, but it's nice for a puffy tied comforter.

Cotton. Cotton batting provides the flat, thin look of an antique quilt. Cotton shrinks slightly when washed, giving it that wrinkled look characteristic of old quilts, so always wash quilts with cotton batting in cold water to prevent excessive shrinking. Most cotton batting should be closely quilted, with quilting lines no more than 1" apart.

Polyester. Look for the word "bonded" when selecting polyester batting. Bonding keeps the loft of the batt uniform and reduces the effects of bearding (the migration of loose fibers through the quilt top). Polyester batting is easy to stitch and can be machine washed with little shrinkage. Avoid bonded batts that feel stiff.

Fleece and Flannel. Fleece is the thinnest of all low-loft batts. It is recommended for use in clothing, table runners, or wall hangings. A single layer of prewashed cotton flannel is good for tablecloths.

Layering

A quilt is a three-layer sandwich held together with quilting stitches. Before you layer the quilt top on the batting and backing, unfold the batting and let it "relax" for a few hours.

Lay backing right side down on a large work surface—a large table, two tables pushed together, or a clean floor. Use masking tape to secure the edges, keeping the backing wrinkle-free and slightly taut.

Smooth the batting over the backing; then trim batting even with the backing. Center the pressed quilt top right side up on the batting. Make sure edges of backing and quilt top are parallel.

Basting

Basting keeps the layers from shifting during quilting. Baste with a long needle and white sewing thread (colored thread can leave a residue on light fabrics).

1 Start in the center and baste a line of stitches to each corner, making a large X. Then baste parallel lines 6"–8" apart. Finish with a line of basting ¼" from each edge of the quilt.

2 Some quilters use nickel-plated safety pins for basting. Pin every 2"–3". Don't close the pins as you go, which can pucker the backing. When all pins are in place, remove the tape at the quilt edges. Gently tug the backing as you close each pin so that pleats don't form underneath.

Quilting

Quilting is the process of stitching the layers of a quilt together, by hand or by machine. The choice of hand or machine quilting depends on the design of the quilt, its intended use, and how much time you want to devote to quilting. The techniques differ, but the results of both are functional and attractive.

Hand Quilting

To quilt by hand, you need a quilting hoop or a frame, quilting thread (which is heavier than sewing thread), quilting needles, and a thimble. If you're not used to a thimble, you'll find it necessary to prevent the quilting needle from digging into your fingertip.

Preparation. Put the basted quilt in a hoop or frame. Start with a size 7 or 8 "between," or quilting needle. (As your skill increases, try a shorter between to make smaller stitches. A higher number indicates a shorter needle.) Thread the needle with 18" of quilting thread and make a small knot in the end.

Tying

Tying is a fast and easy way to secure the quilt layers. It's the best way to work with thick batting for puffy comforters. Tying is also fine for polyester batting, but not for cotton or silk batts, which require close quilting.

For ties, use pearl cotton, lightweight yarn, floss, or narrow ribbon; these are stable enough to stay tightly tied. You'll also need a sharp needle with an eye large enough to accommodate the tie material.

Thread the needle with 6" of thread or yarn. Do not knot the ends. Starting in the center of your basted quilt top, take a small stitch through all three layers. Center a 3"-long tail on each side of the stitch (Diagram 1). Tie the tails in a tight double knot (Diagram 2). Make a tie at least every 6" across the surface of the quilt. Trim the tails of all knots to a uniform length.

Bind the quilt as described on page 156. If your quilt has thick batting, you'll want to cut wider binding strips.

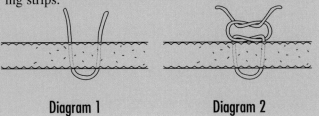

Diagram 1   **Diagram 2**

The Stitch. The quilting stitch is a small running stitch that goes through all three layers of the quilt. Stitches should be small (8–10 per inch), straight, and evenly spaced. Uniformity is more important than the number of stitches per inch. Don't worry if you take only five or six stitches per inch—concentrate on even and straight; tiny comes with practice.

Pop the Knot. Insert the needle through the top about 1" from the point where the quilting will start. Slide the needle through the batting, without piercing the backing, and pull it out where the first stitch will be. Pull the thread taut and tug gently until the knot pops through the top and lodges in the batting (Knot Diagram). If it does not pop through, use your needle to gently separate the fabric threads to let the knot through.

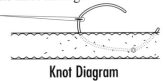

Knot Diagram

Machine Quilting

Choose a small project for your first try at machine quilting, because the bulk of a large quilt can be difficult to manage. Plan simple quilting with continuous straight lines. Good choices are outline or in-the-ditch quilting and allover grids. When you are comfortable with machine quilting, try free-motion quilting and more complex designs.

Preparation. For quilting straight lines, use an even-feed presser foot or a walking foot. You can machine-quilt without this foot, but the work is much easier with it.

Thread the machine with .004 monofilament "invisible" thread or regular sewing thread in a color that coordinates with the quilt. For the bobbin, use sewing thread that matches the backing. Set the stitch length at 8–10 stitches per inch. Adjust the tension so that the bobbin thread does not pull to the top.

Roll the sides of the quilt to the middle and secure the rolls with clips. If you're working on a large quilt, extend your work area by setting up tables to the left and behind the machine to support the quilt while you work.

Straight Lines. Work in long, continuous lines as much as possible. The block seam lines form a grid of long lines across the quilt—quilt these first, starting at the top center and stitching to the opposite edge. Quilt the next line from bottom to top. Alternating the direction of quilting lines keeps the layers from shifting.

Hand Quilting

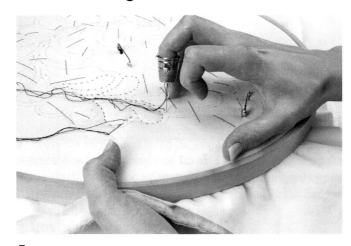

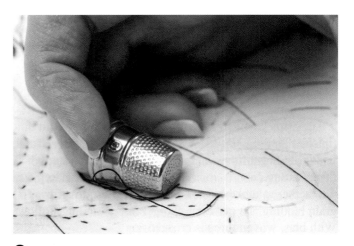

1 **To make a stitch,** first insert the needle straight down. With your other hand under the quilt, feel for the needle point as it pierces the backing. With practice, you'll be able to find the point without pricking your finger.

2 **Roll the needle** to a nearly horizontal position. Use the thumb of your sewing hand and the underneath hand to pinch a little hill in the fabric as you push the needle back through the quilt top. Then rock the needle back to an upright position for the next stitch. Load 3–4 stitches on the needle before pulling it through.

Quilt until you have 6" of thread left. Then tie a knot in the thread close to the quilt top. Take a backstitch and tug to pop the knot into the batting as you did before. Run the thread through the batting and out the top to clip it.

Machine Quilting

1 **Use your hands** to spread the fabric slightly. Gently push the quilt toward the foot to reduce the drag on the fabric. Quilt vertical lines on half the quilt, unrolling it until you reach the edge. Remove the quilt from the machine and reroll it so you can quilt the other half. When all vertical lines are done, reroll the quilt in the other direction to quilt horizontal lines in the same manner.

2 **Following a curved design** is a skill that takes practice and patience to master. Start with a small project that is easy to handle. Attach a darning foot or free-motion quilting foot to your machine. Lower the feed dogs or cover them. You control the stitch length by manually moving the fabric.

Place your hands on each side of the foot so you can maneuver the fabric. To make even stitches, run the machine at a slow, steady speed. Move the fabric smoothly and evenly so that the needle follows the design. Do not rotate the quilt; simply move it forward, backward, and side to side.

Care & Cleaning

A quilt's greatest enemies are light and dirt. To keep your quilt in prime condition would mean never using it. But then you'd never get to see it, enjoy it, or share it. You can enjoy your quilt and still have it last a lifetime if you treat it with care.

Always shield your quilts from direct light and heat, dust, damp, cigarette smoke, and aerosol sprays. The following suggestions for display, storage, and cleaning are suitable for most quilts. A museum-quality heirloom or fragile antique may have special needs; if you have such a quilt, get expert advice on its care.

Washing

Wash your quilts only when absolutely necessary. Often, a good airing is all that's needed to freshen a quilt. Vacuuming with a hose removes dust. Dry cleaning is not recommended for quilts because it leaves harmful chemicals in the fabric.

When you must wash a quilt, use a mild soap such as Ensure or Orvis Paste. These soaps are available at quilt shops and from mail-order catalogs (see page 160).

If you know that a quilt's fabrics were prewashed and tested for colorfastness, you can wash the quilt as described below. If you're not sure, soak a corner of the quilt in lukewarm water to be sure dyes do not bleed.

A Good Soak. If fabrics are prewashed, you can wash your quilt in the washing machine if the machine is large enough to accommodate the quilt. Use cold or lukewarm water and let the machine run through its normal cycles. Never use bleach.

If your quilt is too large for the machine, wash it in the bathtub, letting it soak in warm, soapy water for about 15 minutes. Rinse repeatedly to remove the soap. Squeeze as much water out of the quilt as possible, but don't wring or twist it.

Drying. Carefully lift the quilt out of the washer or tub, supporting the weight of the quilt in your arms so that no part of the quilt is pulled or stressed by the weight of the water. Lay the quilt flat between two layers of towels, and roll it up to remove as much moisture as possible.

Let the quilt dry flat on the floor. If you want to dry it outside, pick a shady spot on a dry day, and place the quilt between sheets to protect it. When the quilt is almost dry, and if it isn't too large, you can put it in the dryer on a cool setting to smooth out wrinkles and fluff it up.

Putting a wet quilt in a clothes dryer is not recommended, because heat and agitation can damage fabric and batting.

Fading

All fabrics fade over time. Some fade faster and more drastically than others, and there's no sure way to identify those fabrics beforehand. However, here is a simple test that is worthwhile if you have time before making a quilt.

Cut a 4" square of each fabric. Tape the squares to a sunny windowpane. After 12 days, compare the squares to the remaining yardage. If the squares are faded to the same degree, you can assume the finished quilt will keep a uniform appearance as it ages. If one fabric fades more than the others, however, you might want to select another for your quilt.

A Breath of Air

By changing the quilt on your bed regularly, you can reduce the damage that exposure will cause to any one quilt. Rotate quilts with the change of each season, for their own good as well as for a fresh look.

All quilts collect dust. Before you put a quilt away for the season, shake it and air it outdoors. A breezy, overcast day is best if the humidity is low. Lay towels on the grass or over a railing; then spread the quilt over the towels. Keep the quilt away from direct sunlight.

Storage

Store quilts in a cool, dry place. Winter cold and summer heat make most attics, basements, and garages inappropriate storage areas.

If you keep a quilt on a rack or in a chest, put several layers of muslin or acid-free paper between the quilt and the wood. A quilt should not be in contact with wood for a long time, as the natural acids in wood will eventually stain the cloth.

To store your quilt, wrap it in a cotton sheet, pillowcase, or acid-free tissue paper. Boxes made of acid-free material are also available (see Mail-Order Resources, page 160). These materials let air circulate but still protect the quilt from dust and damp. Place crumpled acid-free tissue paper inside each fold to prevent stains and creases from developing along fold lines.

Do not store quilts in plastic, which traps moisture and encourages the growth of mildew.

Each time you put a quilt away, fold it differently to prevent damage where fabric fibers become cracked and weak. If possible, avoid folds altogether by rolling the quilt around a tube covered with a cotton sheet.

Glossary of Quiltmaking Terms

Appliqué. From the French word *appliquer,* meaning "to lay on," the process of sewing prepared fabric pieces onto a background fabric to create a layered, pictorial design. Also refers to one piece of the appliqué design.

Backing. The bottom layer of a finished quilt. Can be a single width of fabric or pieced.

Basting. Lines of large, temporary stitches that hold the layers of a quilt together for quilting.

Batting. A soft filling between the patchwork top and the backing.

Bearding. Migration of batting fibers through the quilt top or backing.

Between. A short, small-eyed needle used for hand quilting. Available in several sizes, indicated by numbers; the higher the number, the shorter the needle.

Bias. The diagonal of a woven fabric, which runs at a 45° angle to the selvage. This direction has the most stretch, making it ideal for appliqué shapes and for binding curved edges.

Binding. A narrow strip of folded fabric that covers the raw edges of a quilt after it is quilted.

Bleeding. The run-off of dye when fabric is wet.

Chain piecing. Machine sewing in which units are sewn one after the other without lifting the presser foot or cutting thread between units. Also called assembly-line piecing.

Charm quilt. A quilt composed of one shape in many fabrics. Traditionally, no two pieces are the same fabric.

Contrast. The difference in lightness and darkness of color or size of print.

Cross-hatching. Lines of quilting that form a grid of squares or diamonds.

Crosswise grain. Fabric threads woven from selvage to selvage. Crosswise grain has some stretch, but not as much as bias.

Diagonal corners. A quick-piecing technique that results in a contrasting triangle sewn to one or more corners of a square or rectangle. See page 146 for instructions. Also known as snowball corners.

Easing. A technique used to make unequal pieces match at seams by distributing fullness. See page 145.

Fat eighth. A 9" x 22" cut rather than a standard ⅛ yard (4½" x 44").

Fat quarter. An 18" x 22" cut rather than a standard ¼ yard (9" x 45").

Finished size. Dimensions of a piece or unit when all sides are sewn.

Flying Geese. A basic building block of patchwork, this unit is made of two small triangles sewn to short legs of one large triangle.

Four-Patch. A block made of four squares or units, joined in two rows of two squares each.

Four-triangle square. A pieced square made of four right triangles. Also called an Hourglass block. See technique for quick-piecing these units on page 91.

Grain. The lengthwise and crosswise threads from which fabric is woven. See page 140.

Half-square triangle. A right triangle that results when a fabric square is cut in half diagonally. These triangles are straight grain on the short legs and bias on the hypotenuse.

Hanging sleeve. A fabric casing on the back of a quilt through which a dowel is inserted to hang the quilt on a wall. See page 20.

In-the-ditch. Quilting stitches worked very close to or in the seam line.

Lengthwise grain. Fabric threads parallel to the selvage. Lengthwise grain has very little stretch, if any. Many quiltmakers prefer to cut borders and straight-grain binding on the lengthwise grain.

Nesting. When seam allowances of matching seams fall in opposite directions so that they nest, or fit into one another.

Nine-Patch. A block made of nine squares or units, joined in three rows of three squares each.

Outline quilting. A line of quilting that parallels a seam line, approximately ¼" away.

Pin matching. Using straight pins to align two seams so that they will meet precisely when a joining seam is stitched.

Prairie points. Triangles made from folded squares of fabric that are sewn into seams, creating a dimensional effect. Most often used as an edging. See page 59.

Quarter-square triangle. The right triangle that results when a fabric square is cut in quarters diagonally, in an X. These triangles are bias on the short legs and straight grain on the hypotenuse. Triangles on the outside edge of a diagonal set are cut in this manner to keep the quilt edge on the straight grain.

Quick piecing. One of several machine-sewing techniques that eliminate some marking and cutting steps.

Quilt top. The upper layer of a quilt sandwich, it can be pieced, appliquéd, or wholecloth. Quilting designs are marked and stitched on the top.

Quilting hoop. A portable wooden frame, round or oval, used to hold small portions of a quilt taut for quilting. A quilting hoop is deeper than an embroidery hoop to accommodate the thickness of the quilt layers. Other types of quilting frames, both portable and stationary, are available in a variety of shapes, sizes, and materials.

Quilting stitch. A running stitch that holds the three layers (top, batting, and backing) of a quilt together.

Quilting thread. Heavier than sewing thread, most brands are designed not to snag or snarl.

Reversed patch. A patchwork piece that is a mirror image of another. To cut a reversed patch, turn the template over (reverse it).

Sashing. Strips of fabric sewn between blocks. Also known as lattice stripping.

Sawtooth. A border treatment consisting of two-triangle squares that creates a jagged look.

Selvage. The finished edge of a woven fabric. More tightly woven than the rest of the fabric, selvage is not used for sewing because it shrinks differently when washed.

Set pieces. Elements of a quilt that separate blocks, such as alternate squares, sashing, or side triangles in a diagonal set.

Set-in seam. Where three seams come together in a Y, one piece is set into the two that create the opening. See page 14 for tips on stitching a set-in seam.

Straight grain. The horizontal and vertical threads of a woven fabric. Lengthwise grain runs parallel to the selvage. Crosswise grain is perpendicular to the selvage.

Strip piecing. A quick-piecing technique in which strips of fabric are joined and then cut into segments that become units of a block.

Strip set. A combination of two or more joined strips. These are cut into small segments that become units of patchwork.

Template. A duplicate of a printed pattern, made of sturdy material, that is traced to mark the pattern shape onto fabric.

Triangle-square. A patchwork square made of two or four triangles. When two triangles are joined to make a square, these are called two-triangle squares. When four triangles are joined to make a square, these are called four-triangle squares. Triangles should be cut and sewn so that the straight grain falls on the square's outer edge.

Two-triangle square. A pieced square made of two right triangles. See technique for quick-pieced two-triangle squares on page 148.

Value. The relative lightness or darkness of a color.

Walking foot. A sewing machine foot used for machine quilting and, sometimes, for applying binding. A walking foot feeds a quilt more evenly than a regular foot does.

Mail-Order Resources

Quiltmaking supplies are available at many craft and fabric stores, especially quilting specialty shops. Consult your local telephone directory to find a shop in your area.

If you prefer to have materials delivered to your door, you can order supplies from a mail-order source. The following catalogs are good suppliers of fabric, batting, stencils, notions, and other quilting supplies. All have toll-free telephone numbers and will mail you a catalog at no charge.

Connecting Threads
P.O. Box 8940
Vancouver, WA 98668-8940
(800) 574-6454

Keepsake Quilting
P.O. Box 1618
Centre Harbor, NH 03226
(800) 865-9458

The Quilt Farm
P.O. Box 7877
St. Paul, MN 55107
(800) 435-6201